WOMAN
IN THE
MAKING

R ory O'Neill is Panti Bliss, Ireland's foremost 'gender discombobulist' and accidental activist.

Rory first began performing as his alter-ego Panti when he was an art student in the late '80s before moving to Tokyo and becoming a fixture on the club scene there.

Returning to Dublin in 1995, Panti ran some of Dublin's seminal club nights, hosted the legendary Alternative Miss Ireland for 18 years, and performed all over the world.

Panti has written and performed three critically acclaimed, hit theatre shows: *In These Shoes*, *All Dolled Up* and *A Woman in Progress*. In 2013, *All Dolled Up: Restitched*, a re-imagining of her three hit shows, had a sold-out run at the Abbey Theatre and toured Australia. She is also the landlady of Pantibar.

Panti's creator Rory O'Neill is a champion of gay rights. Dressed with impeccable taste, done up to the nines, and wearing the best (synthetic!) wigs money can buy, he was synonymous with the campaign for equal marriage in Ireland – despite having no plans to wed. This is his first book.

WOMAN
IN THE
MAKING
A MEMOIR

Panti

RORY O'NEILL

HACHETTE
BOOKS
IRELAND

First published in Ireland in 2014 by
HACHETTE BOOKS IRELAND
First published in paperback in 2015

10 9 8 7 6 5 4 3 2 1

A CIP catalogue record for this book is available from the British Library.

ISBN 978 1 44479 857 9

Typeset in Palatino by redrattledesign.com

Printed and bound by Clays Ltd, St Ives plc

Hachette Books Ireland policy is to use papers that are natural, renewable and recyclable products and made from wood grown in sustainable forests. The logging and manufacturing processes are expected to conform to the environmental regulations of the country of origin.

Hachette Books Ireland
8 Castlecourt Centre
Castleknock
Dublin 15, Ireland

A division of Hachette UK Ltd
Carmelite House
50 Victoria Embankment
London EC4Y 0DZ

www.hachette.ie

*To my parents, Rory and Fin O'Neill, who always
let me be whomever I wanted to be.*

Acknowledgements

THIS BOOK WAS WRITTEN UNCOMFORTABLY on planes, trains and automobiles, in snatched moments in dressing rooms and hotel rooms, and in late night bursts with my dog Penny on my lap. That it ever made it to book form at all is some kind of miracle, but that miracle only happened with the invaluable help of other people.

My editor at Hachette Ciara Considine, who first proposed I write this book, mostly managed to hide the panic when I would disappear for days on end, and she adjusted admirably quickly to getting chapters e-mailed to her at 5 a.m. I am indebted to her for her patience, as much as for her advice and guidance.

You wouldn't be reading this book without the poking, prodding, cajoling and advice of my great friend and longtime collaborator Phillip McMahon either, who knows my own stories better than I do. How I ever managed to do anything before I met him I don't remember.

The book wouldn't look as gorgeous as it does without the immense talent and huge patience of graphic designer Niall Sweeney, who hasn't just been a great friend and partner in crime for over twenty years, but has also made Panti look much more beautiful than she really is for over twenty years.

And if you hate this book you can take it up with my agent Faith O'Grady, because apart from encouraging me all the way through, she's the one who got me to agree to do it in the first place.

Prologue

Three days before the paperback edition of this book went to print, Ireland became the first country in the world to introduce marriage equality by popular vote. On Friday 22 May, 2015, the Irish people voted on whether to add seventeen simple words to the constitution: 'Marriage may be contracted in accordance with law by two persons without distinction as to their sex.' And they voted overwhelmingly, 'Yes.'

It came at the end of a tough three-month campaign where the lives and worth of LGBTI people were debated, discussed and weighed, day in day out, on the airwaves, in newspapers, and on doorsteps; our value reduced to slogans on lampposts. It was exhausting, frustrating, mentally draining.

But it was also wonderful. Over those few months, many thousands of ordinary people – gay, straight, and everything in between – joined forces behind a simple idea: that all citizens of the republic should be treated equally under the law. And, to that end, many thousands of people contributed their time, energy and talents. Even if the result had been different, they would have been able to say that they couldn't have done more. They stuffed envelopes, made videos, raised funds and wrote letters. They went to meetings, organised rallies, and got up early to hand out flyers at bus stops and train stations before work. And they talked – to family and co-workers and strangers. They had conversations that weren't always easy, but were necessary. And in groups, that started out small but grew and grew, they attempted to knock on every door in the country – and they almost succeeded! Groups of men and women all across Ireland – students with shaved heads and grandmothers with headscarves, indefatigable activists and groggy-from-night-work taxi drivers – all knocked on the doors of their fellow citizens in pursuit of a simple and beautiful idea: that we are all equally deserving of respect.

And over the course of the campaign, Ireland changed. The cold, unempathetic arguments against equality for gay people were met with hundreds – nay, thousands! – of personal stories from LGBTI people and their families. Stories that were often difficult to tell and painful to hear, but stories that revealed gay people for who we are: real people. And Ireland was moved by them. So moved that, even when the Catholic Church that had loomed so large over my childhood tried to flex its once powerful muscle, the country simply shrugged and looked away.

In truth, the referendum wasn't simply a proposition to extend civil marriage rights to Ireland's gay citizens. By extension, it proposed that lesbian, gay and transgender people are fully equal members of the Irish family, deserving of the respect that everyone else enjoys. And, in the end, the people of Ireland agreed with that simple proposition and our country's LGBTI citizens became full and equal citizens.

As I sit here, writing this epilogue three days later, I am still over the gay moon and drunk on 'yes'. And earlier today, as I walked through Dublin city centre, I saw gay couples casually holding hands as they strolled, and kissing each other goodbye at bus stops in the late spring sunshine, and it seemed to me that was all changed, changed utterly.

Long may it continue.

Rory O'Neill
25 May, 2015

1. Popeular

IN 1979, I STARTED TO think for myself.

It was the year that the Pope came to Ireland, but it was also the year that the eleven-year-old gay boy inside the (till then well-adjusted) eleven-year-old Mayo boy started to act up. These two things were not unrelated.

Looking back now, it seems almost inevitable that my gayness and my Catholicism were about to engage in their first bloody skirmish. After all, this was the year when the Irish chart's top spot was wrestled from 'Mary's Boy Child' by 'YMCA'. But in Ballinrobe, County Mayo in 1979 we simply had no frame of reference for gayness. Gayness was Mr Humphries on *Are You Being Served?* but he lived in the strange, foreign world of TV, not in Ballinrobe.

We certainly did have a frame of reference for popes, though. Indeed, that reference wasn't just framed, it was ornate gilt-framed, hung behind safety glass and expensive lighting.

And this pope was Irish. One of our own. Oh, sure, of course, he was from Poland –

and had a girl's name –

'Carol!'

'*He is* not *called Carol! His name is John Paul the Second!*'

'*He is* now, *but before he was the Pope he was called Carol!*'

'*Feck off you, Damien Fahey, he was not!*'

– a country behind the heathen Iron Curtain, about which we knew nothing, yet we were absolutely sure it was just like Ireland because, like us, they were poor and, like us, they didn't have swanky skyscrapers or Debbie Harry. So John Paul *the Second* would be welcomed with open arms and frantic bunting not just because he was the first pope ever to visit our proudly unswanky island (and long overdue too! Sure weren't we only brilliant at being Catholic?) but because he was practically Irish. He even looked like one of us.

The Pope's itinerary would take him round the country but, ostensibly, the reason for his trip was to visit the small Mayo village of Knock where they were celebrating the centenary of the appearance of the Blessed Virgin Mary herself in that otherwise unremarkable bog village. Knock is not far from Ballinrobe and it had already loomed large and holy in my Mayo childhood, but this was going to be Knock's finest moment!

In truth, though, Knock is the world's worst Marian shrine.

Have you ever been to Lourdes? I have. I was eighteen

years old, and a handsome, muscular Basque gypsy boy with black eyes, pregnant lips, sun-blackened skin and long blue-black hair that whipped in the hot breeze took me there in a beat-up old soft-top. I was in love and lust with him, and the drive through the dramatic Pyrenean mountains to the picturesque fairytale village of Lourdes formed the perfect backdrop to my mostly unrequited love. No one ever rode to Knock in a soft-top with a gypsy boy. For starters, you'd freeze to death. Even the apparition at glamorous picture-postcard Lourdes was so much better than at grey-fog-and-car-park Knock.

In Lourdes, the Virgin pulled out all the stops, all the big special effects – the sun was spinning, water was bubbling up from nowhere, and she kept reappearing to a very strict schedule, whispering very important secrets. In Knock she popped up once, in the middle of the night in the pelting rain, and ruined the drama by bringing a bunch of vaguely recognisable back-up saints. And possibly because of the weather she didn't bring the *actual* Baby Jesus, she brought a lamb. Oh, c'mon, Mary! If you're going to appear in a bog in the middle of the night you could at least bring the Baby Jesus and not a bloody metaphor. And the miracles are so much better in Lourdes! In Lourdes they have these stone baths fed with the icy water from the magic well (they always make such a big deal that no one has ever got an infection from the baths – as if not getting a verruca is somehow miraculous), and the walls of the bathhouse are covered with the discarded crutches of the miraculously cured. It's all very *dramatique*. In Knock, I think they have a pair of old reading glasses and a vague story of someone recovering quite quickly from the flu.

In Knock it's all so literal, so grey. In Lourdes, there's the charming grotto where holy water comes out of gold taps. In Knock, you'd fill your plastic Virgin bottles from aluminium push taps in the car park, and the apparition has been recreated in statue form in front of the pebbledash. (One of my secondary-school classmates, Eugene, claimed his mother had posed for the statue of the Virgin, and I chose to believe him because I thought that one day it would make a nice aside to this story. And I was right. Now when I see that statue of the Virgin I wonder what Eugene is up to these days.)

But now the Pope was coming and this wasn't just going to be the greatest thing that had ever happened to Knock, it was going to be the greatest thing that had ever happened to Ireland! The Pope himself, this huge holy celebrity, was coming and nothing would ever be the same again. At least a million people would go to see him in the Phoenix Park, and at the youth mass in Galway, uncynical, unrebellious young people would gather in their hundreds of happy-clappy thousands to 'Kumbaya, my Lord, kumbaya'.

There were no dissenting voices – or if there were, I was certainly too young to hear them. Everyone was on board.

Even I was on board. After all, I was already putting my latent drag tendencies to work as Ballinrobe's pre-eminent altar (lady) boy. Indeed, my butter-wouldn't-melt look, my theatrical sense of showy detail, and my onstage demeanour (pious, ostentatiously humble, but never pulling focus from the main players) meant I was much in demand for weddings (where I was handsomely rewarded in cash by the happy couple) and Easter services up in the Convent (where I was less handsomely rewarded by the soapy-smelling nuns).

But even my enthusiasm, driven as it was by the perceived glamour of the occasion, paled into insignificance beside my devout mother's papal devotion. For days beforehand, our house, like every other house in Ballinrobe, was a hive of activity and nervous excitement, my mother a sandwich-making tweedy blur. At the crack of dawn on the big day she piled the Volkswagen high with egg sandwiches, brown bread, flasks of tea, 'Pope stools', Holy See flags, my sisters Edel and Clare, and me, and drove to the next town, Claremorris, where we parked in a field. (Claremorris is fifteen miles from Ballinrobe, and was Ballinrobe's nemesis. They had a swimming pool and a railway station, and their school marching band had more stylish uniforms than ours, but we had a cattle mart, a one-way traffic system, water towers that looked like a pair of boobs, and our marching band just so happened to have won the Connaught regional title, thank you very much, with no small help from a stylish turn on the glockenspiel by, yes, that's right, Ballinrobe's pre-eminent altar boy! Last Christmas my father picked me up from the station in Claremorris. After ten minutes I remarked that we still hadn't managed to get out of the small rural town because of the traffic, and he spat, 'Ah, sure it's always shite in Claremorris. Those feckers have always thought they can just park anywhere they like. All over the road!')

At Claremorris we boarded shuttle buses to the site at Knock, where we were herded into our assigned corrals. In the grey early-morning light it was a sight to behold – hundreds of thousands of damp pilgrims, their breath clouding the frigid air, muttering their bovine devotions, stretched out across endless moist fields, ironically vacated by their actual bovine residents for the glorious occasion.

Keeping us children close, my mother led the way (it was just our mother and us smaller kids – our older siblings would be going to see the Pope at the Youth Mass in Galway, and my father was somewhere among the glorious throng where he was working as a volunteer steward) till we set up camp miles from the stage, among nodding nuns, stressed mothers, praying shopkeepers, and farmers drinking cold tea from TK lemonade bottles, as an interminable tinny rosary bleated over the Tannoy system.

The hours dragged damply by, and as we waited for the Pope's arrival we ate our soggy sandwiches, and considered wetting ourselves rather than risk life and infection by going to the toilets – you had to balance on slippery wooden planks above a hole in the ground already filled with the piss and shit of hundreds of holy pilgrims. And there is nothing like the stench of other people's faeces to disabuse you of the notion that anything spiritual might be happening.

By the time the Pope arrived – or, at least, the tiny distant dot that sounded like him and everyone insisted *was* him, despite no real evidence (like good Catholics, we were just going to have to take it on faith) – it already felt like we'd been at a mass for days on end, but now an actual mass started. It was longer and more boring than any mass I'd ever been to.

However, by the time it ended, the excitement was almost palpable, because this was what everyone was really waiting for – the Popemobile! It's impossible to grasp now but, at the time, the Popemobile was this *huge* deal, a triumph of marketing achieved by the simple act of swapping the word 'bat' for 'pope'. For weeks beforehand we had talked of nothing else in the schoolyard after seeing a report on children's TV about it being built. It was basically just a jeep with a bulletproof glass box at the back that the Pope would be driven through the crowds in, but the way people went on you'd swear it was the *Starship Enterprise*!

At the end of the mass the Pope would drive through the corrals of people, and it was our chance to get up quite close to him and take the shaky photograph that would be treasured for years to come. But then it was announced over the Tannoy that because things were running behind schedule, and it was already getting dark, the Pope was going to leave immediately. He might have been God's chosen representative on earth, successor to St Peter, with a direct line to the Virgin – but he still had to be home in time for *Coronation Street*.

Everyone was crushed. On the verge of tears, nuns looked at each other with stricken faces, and my mother shrivelled before my very eyes. Hundreds of thousands of cold, wet people looked at each other, said, 'Feck this crap,' and left. All at the same time. In the dark. It was total chaos. There was no way they could get the buses through the frustrated throngs, so everyone had to walk the eight miles back to Claremorris, down tiny Mayo country roads, in the pitch dark, jostled by hundreds of thousands of other people. My mother, cold, wet and miserable, made us kids, cold, wet, miserable, tired and cranky, hold hands as we stumbled and bumped the eight miles back to the car, my little sister Clare crying all the way. It was a frightening experience. Treasured Pope stools were tossed into ditches, exasperated parents tugged at small, exhausted hands, and my mother, even in the dark, looked tired, and disappointed, and, to me, for the first time in my life, like a *real* person, with all the fragilities that that implies.

On the drive home from Claremorris, I was exhausted in the back seat, but I couldn't sleep. My mother's hands were illuminated by the light from the dashboard – her knuckles were white as she gripped the steering wheel, and I could see the blood in her veins. I'd never even noticed she had veins before.

The Pope's visit made me think – really think – for the very first time.

During the interminable mass I had looked around me and had an epiphany of sorts. I didn't belong there. I looked at the hundreds of thousands of people muttering as one and I didn't feel any wonder. I felt no joy. I felt afraid. There was nothing spiritual or divine about the event: this was a cult. A cult of personality and hype. A passive mob, a colony of drones; a multicellular organism made up of unicellular minds. A switching off of all critical faculties. And had I had the eleven-year-old courage I would have stood up and screamed, 'The Pope has no clothes!' (Which might very well have been true but he was so far away it was impossible to discern.)

It made me question what was presented to me. Made me wary of accepted truths. That day, a crack opened up between me and the world around me. A crack that over the years became a crevasse, then a gorge, and then a chasm. It's a chasm I've come to treasure. The Pope's visit unhooked me from the dead weight of religion and pushed me into the stream of my own consciousness. It gave me a mind of my own.

I didn't become an atheist that day – that was a much longer process – but I did take the first step, and became a Protestant.

2. Small-town Boy

I THINK SOMETIMES WHEN PEOPLE look at me, this big painted 'lady', they find it hard to imagine that I came from anywhere. They imagine that I just appeared, fully formed, like the Good Witch Glinda from her bubble. But, of course, I am from somewhere – a small town in the West of Ireland.

Ballinrobe is your typical Irish country market town. It has a couple of streets, a church, a town hall, a cattle mart, and there was great excitement when Tesco arrived. And even though it now has a Tesco, it hasn't really changed much since I was growing up there, a boy called Rory, in the 1970s.

Growing up in 1970s Ballinrobe, the much-loved son of the local vet and his well-respected wife, surrounded by five noisy brothers and sisters and countless animals, it was idyllic: easy, free, fun. The weather seemed better than now, the summers longer. All my most vivid and immediate memories are of warm sunny days, poking things with sticks or pulling the seeds off tall blades of grass in one stroke between your fingers so they form a precarious flower on your fingertips. Our parents had built our house in 1967, a modern 'architect-designed' (that was always important) flat-roofed bungalow on a large plot of land right at the edge of the town, down a tiny narrow lane known as the Bog Road, just off one of the main streets. For many years the only other residents of the Bog Road (though some gardens and sheds of other houses backed onto it) were the dead souls in the overgrown ancient graveyard next door, with its crumbling, spooky ruined abbey, and past that, the Traveller families in their caravans. They called the Bog Road home all year round and came to our house every day looking for the boss or the missus, depending on what they wanted.

There were technically only six O'Neill children, but our big garden, with easy access to the fields, woods and slow-moving river behind it, meant our house was a Mecca for other local kids, some of whom became indistinguishable from our actual siblings. Eve, whose own house backed onto the Bog Road, was as likely to be eating dinner in our house as her own, and my brother's friend Denny ended up living with us for a number of years after his parents died and is still a brother to us.

During the school holidays, we'd go out in the morning and spend the day exploring the woods, swimming in the lake, scrambling over rivers, or playing 'Grace O'Malley Pirate Queen' in the neglected graveyard, as we sailed our tombstone pirate ships through the undergrowth and leaped aboard those of our hapless victims, with bloodcurdling pirate screams. Later we sat on the same lichen-covered slabs, ate jam sandwiches and talked about the time Sparks Guckian had found a skull in the bushes even though none of us had actually seen it. But he had.

You'd be gone all day and your mother wouldn't worry or care where you were as long as you were back by teatime with all your fingers and toes. Even now, they have an admirably relaxed attitude to child safety in County Mayo. Like the rest of the country, every Mayo garden seems to have sprouted a trampoline in the last few years, but in Mayo nobody has a safety net round it. My own sister's family have one that sits awkwardly on the edge of the bone-shattering tarmacadam driveway while my nieces and nephew and their friends are catapulted in every direction at the speed of broken collar bones. But sure they'll be grand. (And they are.)

As a vet's family we were always surrounded by animals – dogs, cats, budgies, rabbits, sheep, ponies, chickens, hedgehogs … We adopted most of them, strays or foundlings that appeared one day and never left. Some adopted us. On more than one occasion my father attended to an animal that then simply refused to return to its original owners, cleaving instead to him. Tiger Ryder, a farting, slightly bad-tempered wire-haired terrier who belonged to the Ryder family up the road, was brought to my dad after he'd been badly attacked by a large dog. Dad patched him up and spoke to him in the way he has with animals, and every morning thereafter we'd find Tiger Ryder on our doorstep and nothing could keep him away. So Tiger Ryder became an O'Neill, even though he never changed his name.

There were no rules about the animals because there didn't need to be. The house was big enough, with its sprawling garden and little copse of trees, so the animals, like the kids, came and went as they pleased. But we were a country vet's family so we weren't sentimental about them. They were part of the family, wandering in and out as they pleased and falling asleep in front of *Hill Street Blues* on the TV like the rest of us. Apart from little funerals and occasionally a tombstone at the bottom of the garden when they passed away, they were just animals. They ate dog food and left-overs and were largely ignored till all hell broke loose when my father arrived home from work.

To enable us to make pocket money (and teach us some kind of responsibility) my dad would buy my brother and me a bull calf each (Barney and Beany, or Ernie and Bert) to look after. Every morning before school we'd mix up their feed and shiver in the morning mist watching their noisy, mucousy breath clouds and letting them suck and chew wetly on our fingers till I worried they would suck them right off. When they were a year old Dad would take them to the mart and sell them. After deducting what he'd paid for them and their feed, we'd get to keep the profit.

School was a walk away. (On rainy days we'd ask our dad for a lift and he'd say, 'You're not a lump of sugar – you won't melt!' Eventually we'd only ask to hear him say it.) The crumbling cinema showed double bills and I fell in love with child star Jodie Foster. I got stung on the tongue by a wasp while eating an apple at the lake and it swelled up so that I had to call my mother from the phone box to come and get me. On Bonfire Night my dad would cook sausages on a dirty shovel and we'd eat them and think they were the best sausages ever. I told the teacher in front of the whole class that I didn't like football; he and the other kids looked at me like I was speaking a foreign language. And one time I was cycling along the river path and a guy went to cast out a fishing line without seeing me and the hook caught in my hand.

There's a lot to be said for growing up in Ballinrobe, County Mayo.

The one thing Mayo didn't have was glamour. It had grass and cows, fish and football, but no glamour. Glamour was in short supply in 1970s Ireland anyway, and what little there was rarely made it past the Shannon, and usually came from abroad. When Mrs Nixon, the wife of the disgraced president, came to Ballinrobe in a helicopter and shook hands with people at the local agricultural show, the whole town nearly had a stroke. She was like something out of a 'fillim'.

But glamour came to our house once every few years in the shape of Aunty Qy, my mother's younger sister. She even had a glamorous name; Columba, which everyone shortened to Q or Qy for some reason. Aunty Qy. She was gorgeous, and had this rich, husky voice, redolent of Katharine Hepburn's. She had wanted to be an actress, and did a bit on radio, but mostly she was just beautiful. Seven different men proposed to her and in fact my mother met my father when he came to the house to take Aunty Qy out. But Aunty Qy said no to all her suitors until a wealthy American, an ex-naval officer, proposed. He was twenty-five years her senior, but he was dashing and exciting, and in grey 1950s Ireland, he was in Technicolor, and he took her to America.

In 1970s Ireland, America still retained a sense of real glamour. It was a faraway exotic place we'd probably never see, where Mary Tyler Moore and Charlie's Angels lived with giant refrigerators and bouncing hair. Aunty Qy would arrive home with her husky drawl, in a swirl of beige pantsuits and menthol cigarettes (cigarettes *with mint in them*!) and the glamour would almost knock me over. She'd smoke and drawl and sing, 'I'm a Woman' and her bracelets would clank as she'd take out gifts wrapped like they were in American movies, with shiny paper and glittery bows, and inside we'd discover new and amazing things: Pez dispensers, magic tricks, a jumper *with a hood on it*! America had everything! We'd never seen the like! The whole town was talking about us and our jumpers with the hoods.

All the other kids wanted to have an aunty Qy. I wanted to *be* Aunty Qy.

She was like no one else I'd ever met. She was exotic and glamorous and *different*. She was like a character from a movie, a 3D emissary from a 2D world I'd only ever seen on screen or in books. But she was flesh and blood, undeniable tangible evidence of a big world out there, somewhere past Roscommon. I feverishly imagined this other world and fevered to be part of it. This bigger, brighter world full of new and different things, exciting and full of possibilities – where people wore jumpers with hoods on them.

3. Chalk Dust and Habits

NUNS, CHRISTIAN BROTHERS, FRANCISCANS: THESE monochromatic figures took charge of my education from when I was four, hovering through my childhood like *Star Wars* extras who'd wandered onto the wrong set, smelling of soap and the chalk dust that clung to their robes, like stains left by passing clouds.

Like every other child in Ballinrobe, at four years old I went to the Convent where, for three years, Sisters of Mercy with made-up names, like Sister Alphonsus or Sister Gertrude (I knew these couldn't actually be real names: they were comedy names, like the generic 'Sister Mary Ramsbottom', who starred in every joke my father told that called for a nun, as most of his jokes did), taught me reading, writing, Irish and 'sums'. They also prepared me for my First Holy Communion, an event that was clearly meant to have great significance but was entirely wasted on six-year-old me. I remember it only because my mother made me a suit, and after the boring church bit we had a party with cake and sandwiches in the school hall, where the girls jealously guarded their little white handbags with their 'communion money' in them.

For mysterious reasons I neither understood nor appreciated, making your First Holy Communion also meant that the boys would be separated from the girls. While the girls would remain with the nuns in the relatively modern convent school, we boys would move across town to the old grey stone buildings and cheap, felt-roofed prefabs that made up the Christian Brothers boys' school. The buildings – classrooms, toilet, bike shed – huddled round a stark yard in the shadow of the town's Catholic church, which, to all intents and purposes, was the town's only church. There was a Protestant church, too, but it sat mostly hidden down a lane, barely impinging on the town's consciousness, and I never saw a soul coming or going – though whether Protestants actually even had souls was still up for discussion because they'd never made their First Holy Communion.

The school's reputation hung heavy, particularly with the principal, an angry, violent, un-Christian Brother: he beat boys who failed to memorise the words to the national anthem, or otherwise transgressed, with the 'Leather' – a piece of thick, sewn leather that was, incredibly, made specially for grown men to beat children with. And that reputation was mostly deserved, though there were good, kind lay teachers, too. Thankfully for me, by the time I reached the dreaded principal's sixth class he had been replaced by another brother who was less quick to take out the Leather, and even less so after an angry parent burst into the classroom one day and violently confronted him in front of thirty open-mouthed boys. The Traveller boy who shared the desk with me poked me in the ribs and pinched himself so he didn't jump up and cheer.

When I was twelve and finished primary school, a decision needed to be made. One option was to stay in Ballinrobe and move to the Big School, which had a reputation for boozy teachers, crumbling buildings and an uninspiring track record of academic achievement. Whether this reputation was wholly deserved or not, I don't know, but the twelve-year-old me viewed it with suspicion and some trepidation. It seemed depressing and shabby, the 'big' boys seemed rough and everyone said that one of them had blown up a prefab in chemistry class.

The other option was that I could follow my two older brothers and go to a boarding school run by Franciscans on the east coast near where my grandparents lived. We had grown up visiting them in their little house on the sandy beach. My parents assumed I would go, and I assumed I would go. In fact, I wanted to go. I was already beginning to be aware that I didn't feel I really belonged in Ballinrobe. It was a vague feeling because I had no real experience of other places and therefore no real idea of somewhere I might feel less ... on the outside. But I felt it. I wasn't exactly unhappy – I had friends, I painted pictures and made models out of plaster. I built the world's worst barbecue at the bottom of the garden and left it unfinished for years. My parents (in an act of parental encouragement both wonderful and foolhardy) let me paint the whole of the long corridor in the house with bucolic scenes of Swiss mountains and cable cars filled with excited skiers (I had never even seen skis, let alone been skiing). I liked cycling down to the lake on hot days and diving into the dark bog water from the pier while the women of the town sat chest-high in the water, washed their hair and chatted.

And yet I was lonely. The kinds of things I was becoming interested in – drawing pictures, being one of Charlie's Angels, Tony Danza – weren't things my friends were interested in and I felt myself becoming more distant. I imagined myself far away from Ballinrobe, bounding from a cable car in the Alps, wearing a jumper with a hood, or 'shooting the breeze' with the rest of the Angels as we sat around the intercom, then got caught in freeze-frame, laughing at Charlie's latest quip with our heads thrown back and our Californian hair caught in shiny mid-bounce.

Going to boarding school seemed a start. There'd be people from places other than Ballinrobe, and sure hadn't my eldest brother Lorcan already left the school early, having won a scholarship to go to a weird but amazing-sounding international school on an island off Canada. There he learned weird subjects and did sea rescue, and all the students were on scholarships and came from all over the world. That was definitely somewhere else and sounded so much better than secondary school with chalk-dusty Christian Brothers in Ballinrobe.

And my other brother, Fergal, he'd still be there and that would definitely make it much easier, right? Wrong. It turned out that Fergal was terribly homesick all the time and hated being constantly compared to our super-smart eldest brother, who'd gone off to Canada –

'On his own?'

'On his own.'

'Without a murmur?'

'Without a murmur.'

'When he was fifteen?'

'Only fifteen.'

'Well, isn't that something now!'

'It's something all right.'

– so he begged my parents to let him come home and go to school in Ballinrobe. And just before I was supposed to go, he did.

Suddenly I wasn't at all convinced that I wanted to go. Now that Fergal wouldn't be there I'd be all alone and would know nobody. What if I was homesick and hated it, too? Actually, no 'if'. I was *definitely* going to hate it. I'd be miserable and the whole thing was a crazy idea – and I don't care what Mammy says, I'm not going, and if Lindsay Wagner, who plays Jaime Sommers, a.k.a. the Bionic Woman, was here she'd totally agree.

But then my eldest sister Auveen sat me down and she was my big sister and she had glamorous long-haired friends from Westport, who sometimes came to the house and smelt nice and flicked their hair, and she was the only one of the girls who'd gone to boarding school so she knew what it was like and she knew me and she just knew I'd like it and it'd be good for me, and won't I at least go to the 'entrance exam' and see how I feel about it then because what's the harm in that, and if I still don't want to go after that, well, fine, nobody will make me, all right?

So I went to the entrance exam over a couple of days where, apart from sitting a few easy multiple-choice tests, it was like a holiday camp. We played games and ran around and I made friends with boys with funny accents from places I'd never heard of, like Trim and Balbriggan and Dundalk, and even the brown-robed Franciscans seemed nicer than the black-robed Christian Brothers, and one of them even had a huge, drooling St Bernard dog. There was an impressive front gate with a mosaic of St Francis and an imposing long driveway lined with trees that led to a castle where apparently the monks actually lived! There was a swimming pool – a proper swimming pool! A real one with tiles! Not like the cold, dank, above-ground slimy wooden thing we'd driven fifteen miles to in Claremorris every week, crammed into the back of our car or Mrs Mayes's car to have proper swimming lessons so we wouldn't all drown when we went to the lake on our own in the summer.

I loved it.

And I was conned.

Not that I hated it and had a terrible time – I didn't. My sister was right, boarding school did suit me, but the weekend had been a lie. We were never allowed near the 'castle' – only boys in senior year were allowed out the front with its impressive grounds – there was very little running around, we rarely saw the drooling St Bernard, and it turned out that the swimming pool was no place for splashing about, O'Neill! No place for wobble-swimming under water, pretending to be handsome Patrick Duffy in *The Man from Atlantis* in his little yellow trunks. The pool was for aggressive throat-screaming water polo matches or training till you puked.

Boarding school is Darwinism in action: survival of the fittest. The strong survive and thrive while the weak are cruelly crushed, and traits unhelpful to survival, like fatness or Dungeons & Dragons or an interest in an insufficiently heterosexual pop star are bred out of the gene pool through relentless mocking. Which should have boded ill for me, with my interest in art (definitely considered suspiciously gay), my lack of interest in field sports (gay and weird), and my well-worn copy of Wham!'s first album (on cassette, a medium still so new that the record company hadn't bothered to make a rectangular version of the album artwork so the bottom third of the cassette cover was just a lazy white stripe).

And yet boarding school still suited me. I was the kind of confident, mouthy kid who got on fine with the rowdy football types, but with enough nerdy qualities to get on with the studious dragon-slayer who had a burning desire to be a chartered accountant. I'd happily play Dungeons & Dragons after class with the nerds, and before bed smoke cigarettes in the toilet while entertaining the other smokers with my campy, slinky rendition of 'I'm a Woman'.

But some boys simply weren't the right personality type for boarding school and should never have been there. Boarding school is like prison: even though the inmates are constantly supervised, they develop their own crude society, with its own code, under the noses of the guards. And when the inmates are five hundred teenage boys away from Mammy for the first time, that code can be sometimes brutal and often cruel.

Some boys were simply cripplingly homesick and would never grow out of it. They walked around the school with slumped shoulders and drawn faces, and at night you'd sometimes hear the lonely sound of their blanket-muffled sobs. Others made the fatal mistake of showing a weakness. Or being fat. Or thin. Or ginger. Or awkward. Or buck-toothed or curly-haired or big-lipped or funny-named or green-eyed or any other seemingly arbitrary thing that the pack decided to turn against. And the pack could be relentless. There were boys who went through years of torture; leaving them there to endure it was stupid and cruel. I suppose it's possible that some of them now look back and think it made them stronger people – but I doubt it.

And then there were the alpha-boys: the football team, the rowdy lads, the 'cornerboys' (as our classical-studies teacher, Mr Seavers, had it), the early shavers, who sat atop this volatile teenage flesh pyramid and beat their boy-man chests. No doubt some of those boys went on to great success later in life, but for many this was their peak. Their particular collection of personality traits and talents perfectly suited the somewhat primitive society of boarding school, and they ruled like demi-gods; once they were released into the real world they found they needed a whole other set of skills they simply didn't have.

These were the kind of boys who, years later, would call into the school as 'past pupils' to have a look at the old place and relive their triumphs. The kind of wistful men who'd occasionally interrupt one of our classes to reminisce with the monk who was teaching us: 'Oh, I was just passing, Father, and thought I'd pop in to see the old place,' a nostalgic half-smile wrinkling their still-new crow's feet. They'd wander the corridors remarking how small everything looked and exclaiming that the fish tank was still there! After they left, Father Declan would tell us that one day we'd look back and realise that these were the best days of our lives, and I would think, Fuck.

If these are the best days of my life I'm going to kill myself.

But for me, although boarding school was annoying and boring, it was bearable. It quite suited me. I was always very independent and self-contained and (I think to my mother's secret disappointment) I never had a single moment's homesickness. I was a lazy and poorly organised student, but I was naturally book-smart so coasted along with reasonable grades without much effort. I got on with pretty much everybody, pupils and staff, and although I was often in trouble as I got older, there was never any malice in me – I was simply testing the boundaries of my limited freedoms. And my 'gang' were similar types, as happy to smoke cigarettes and sneak off school grounds as to represent the school in a classical-studies competition with a homoerotic wall project on Perseus.

Often when I mention to people that I went to an all-boys boarding school they raise a knowing eyebrow because they've seen all that *Brideshead Revisited* / English public school / Rupert Everett / blowjobs 'n' bumming stuff. No doubt boarding school was just one long sword fight with teenage erections so hard they could cut glass, right? But I have to disappoint them: a Franciscan boarding school outside Balbriggan is a far, sexually repressed, cry from Eton 'fags' and Guy Burgess.

Any hint of sexuality of any sort was cause for alarm. The Franciscans were like Carrie's mum, aware of the awesome, unpredictable power of burgeoning teen sexuality and terrified that if even a little escaped it could run amok, becoming more and more powerful and impossible to control till it destroyed the school dance and killed John Travolta. And how terrifying it must have been for them when every year a new influx of healthy, soon-to-be-horny young boys on the cusp of puberty arrived, full of raging hormones and confusing dreams about Farrah Fawcett. Was one of these fresh-faced young boys the soon-to-be-acne-faced sexual terrorist with a backpack of hormones so explosive they might destroy the school?

But while the school was terrified of any suggestion of sexuality among the boys, the main fear was, of course, homosexuality – the bumming that dare not speak its name. Not only because homosexuality was A HORRIBLE CRIME AGAINST GOD AND AGAINST NATURE but because unlike heterosex, homosex was an actual real-live possibility. After all, here were five hundred boys with boundless energy, hair sprouting in new places, and not a pair of X chromosomes as far as the eye could see. To all intents and purposes, we were living in a Sahara of penis, a tundra of testosterone, where no oestrogen bloomed. (It wasn't strictly true. There was an attractive lady biology teacher, but we only ever saw her in class, and local women worked in the canteen, throwing beans onto our plates from the other side of a hatch, but in their shapeless overalls and funny hats they seemed less like women and more like sitcom characters.)

The school's main strategy in the war against homosex was never to allow any privacy of any kind. Twenty-four hours a day, seven days a week, we were surrounded by other boys or supervised by adults, and usually both. We slept in huge dormitories the size of aircraft hangars where rows of beds formed long corridors that seemed to stretch to a vanishing point. At night the pale light from the curtainless windows would pattern the parquet floor and the quiet squeak of leather sandals would timidly announce the passing of a shadowy monk by the end of your bed, as the priest or brother on dorm duty made his rounds. Hanging high on the wall at the end of every dorm, looming over us like a gruesome horror-movie prop, was a life-sized plaster crucified Jesus, his bony ribs sticking through his grey-painted death-pallor skin, livid red blood pouring into his eyes from his crown of thorns, and – in a detail all too real for a twelve-year-old boy – the skin scraped painfully off his bloody knees. (I can only assume that an unusually high number of ex-pupils must have ended up paying prostitutes to tie them up and beat them.)

Our days were spent in Clearasil-smelling herds, prodded from dorm to canteen (there's bloody Jesus again) to class (hello again, gruesome Jesus) to football field (phew!) to study hall (there he is again). So even if two horny, confused, excited farmers' sons wanted to compare erections, the opportunities to do so in peace were very few and very far between. Oh, I'm sure they did from time to time – that's what hormone-addled boys in all-male environments do and, as Jeff Goldblum astutely points out in *Jurassic Park*, 'Life finds a way' – but it certainly wasn't common and most certainly wasn't boasted about.

In my own case it only ever happened with one boy that I remember. He was one of the alpha-males, a popular member of the Gaelic team, and during second year, out of the blue, he appeared in the dark during the night and sat on my bed and we clumsily and silently rubbed each other's erections. I don't even remember if we kissed or even if we fellated each other, but I do remember the musky, slightly acrid smell of his skin so I guess I kissed something. It happened a couple more times after that, the same way. But he was one of those boys who never got over the homesickness, and although he was a tough guy during the day, at night he'd often cry himself to sleep. After one summer holiday he didn't come back. Mostly my homosexuality was confined to occasional crushes on handsome older boys about whom I'd occasionally have cheesy romantic Mills & Boon fantasies, and about whom I'd occasionally masturbate.

At some point every year the first-years (or 'preps') would go through a 'bender' phase, even though we only had the vaguest idea of what homosexuals were or did. For a short time all the jokes would be about homos –

'Did you hear there's a queer in our year?'
'Who?'
'Give us a kiss and I'll tell ya!'

– and before 'lights out' the dormitory would be filled with homoerotic grappling, 'pile-ons', with studiously ignored hard-ons, and good-natured claims and counterclaims of 'Bender!' and 'Puff!' And then, as quickly as it started, it would pass and never be mentioned again. Till next year's first-years had their bender phase.

And yet, even in this repressed, sexually innocent atmosphere, everyone knew what went on in Father Ronald's office. The pupils knew, the other Franciscans knew, the staff knew. Everyone knew.

There were a couple of priests or brothers who had reputations for being a bit too touchy-feely, but for the most part it seemed fairly benign – lonely unmarried men who perhaps enjoyed a hug as a fairly rare moment of human contact. But Father Ronald was different.

Father Ronald was a balding, grey-haired, chubby man in his fifties with thick-rimmed glasses, who, among other things, was the school bursar (if you needed money you would go to his office and plead your case, and he would debit your account in a little notebook) and, bizarrely, the school sex-education teacher. Every boy in the school was occasionally called to Father Ronald's office for 'the talk'. His voice would come over the Tannoy system during 'study', and as the named boy got up from his desk to make his way out of the hall, two hundred boys would pull rapidly at their cheeks making a masturbation sound while the friar on duty glared down at us till silence was restored. After 'study' when the boy was back, we'd gather round and ask him if Father Ronald had touched him, and if he had what he'd done, and laugh about it because we didn't know what else we were supposed to do.

For me and my friends, Father Ronald was little more than a creepy unpleasantness. A necessary evil. I would realise I needed money for something and, with the resigned dread of a poorly prepared student going to an exam, I would slouch to his office, press the buzzer and watch the little traffic lights that were outside his and all the other friars' offices. If the red light came on it meant, 'Go away, I'm busy'. If the orange light came on it meant, 'Wait a minute', and if the green light came on it meant, 'Come in'. For the most part I escaped unscathed from my visits to Father Ronald's office. Once, during one of my two sex-education 'talks', he asked me if my friends and I ever pulled each other's Speedos down in the pool, told me we should shower naked together, then demonstrated how I should tuck my shirt, pushing my shirt tail into my underpants with his meaty hands. It was creepy, uncomfortable and embarrassing, but afterwards I told my friends about it and we joked and made puking noises about Ronnie the Bender.

Other boys were not so lucky. We all knew that Father Ronald paid particular attention to certain boys, but the details were vague. Those boys didn't laugh and joke about it, and some innate sense in us told us not to ask. Once, one of the quietest, most naïve, most sheltered boys in the school, who wore ironed slacks every day, had no real friends and spoke to his mother on the phone every evening (it was rumoured she told him what clothes to wear the next day), came back into the study hall after a visit to Father Ronald's office and, as usual, we all started to make masturbation sounds. Until we realised the boy was sobbing crying. And the cacophony of stupid masturbation sounds subsided till all that was left was a confused, embarrassed silence, punctuated by a lonely boy's stifled sobs.

Sex and sexuality were just too confusing and too alien in school to deal with properly, so for the most part I simply ignored them. Of course, as I went through my teenage years I started to suspect I might be gay, but it was still such an alien concept, so foreign, so removed from my actual experience, that I mostly buried these uncomfortable suspicions. I'd never met or even, for sure, *seen* a real, actual, bona fide homosexual so the idea that I might actually *be* one was almost impossible to process. I might equally have wondered if I were a unicorn. I wasn't totally sure gays *actually* existed. I couldn't be entirely sure they weren't just made up, invented to be the subject of schoolyard jokes and played for smutty laughs on sitcoms.

There were no gays in my world. No hairdresser with trendy tattoos in my mother's local salon, no lesbian couple breeding dogs on my father's client list, no Graham Nortons being casually gay on the telly, no Will Youngs singing about boyfriends on the radio, no Anna Nolans being a 'lesbian nun' on *Big Brother*. Even my toothy, tanned, big-haired and short-shorted George Michael was straight. There was only Mr Humphries, swishing and flapping his way through Grace Brothers' department store leaving a trail of canned laughter in his wake.

There were, of course, gays to be seen on TV and in magazines, but either they didn't identify themselves as gay or we simply didn't recognise them as such. When Village People appeared on the telly in the late seventies, the boys of Ballinrobe's Christian Brothers primary school just thought of them as a gang of fun guys in crazy outfits. We simply had no frame of reference for leather queens. When Boy George first appeared on *Top of the Pops*, the next day in the schoolyard the big discussion was whether he was a girl or a boy – the idea that he might simply be a flaming queen never entered our minds. It may seem incredible now that we didn't simply assume Larry Grayson or Kenny Everett or Vincent Hanley were gay, but they weren't casually referring to hot guys on chat shows or discussing husbands in the TV guide, and what did an eleven-year-old boy in Ballinrobe, County Mayo, know about moustaches or check shirts or faded jeans or any of the other tell-tale signs of urban homosexuality? Absolutely nothing.

It was my parents' library that first confirmed for me the existence of gay men. Among the books I discovered a yellow-paged, dog-eared copy of *The Naked Ape* by zoologist Desmond Morris. Morris's book was one of the first popular science books to look at humans as an animal species and compare them to other animals and, as any curious boy would, I skipped the boring parts and went straight to the chapter on sexuality. Within that chapter there was a section on homosexuality, a revelation to pubescent me. Morris described calmly and matter-of-factly what homosexuals were and what they did. There were some dodgy 1960s Freudian comments on what might cause homosexuality in males (domineering mothers, weak fathers, etc.), but other than that, he mostly presented gays as facts rather than opinions. There was no judgement. For the first time ever, not only did I have solid proof that gay people existed but, even more thrillingly, here was someone – an obviously smart and respected man – who wasn't laughing at homosexuals, judging them or denouncing them. He was simply describing them. In fact he went as far as to say that, from a detached zoological perspective, there was nothing to judge and that, in some particular situations, it could even be argued that homosexuality was biologically 'moral'. It excited me so much that I read it over and over again, sexually aroused and intellectually giddy. Here was *what* I was, reflected back at me in black and yellowed white, and it was as thrilling as it was terrifying. So terrifying that I'd slam the book shut, shove it back under my bed and try to forget about it till the next time I crawled under to get it with my heart in my gay mouth.

But in school I pushed all that to the back of my mind and got on with the boring business of being a schoolboy. However, that didn't stop the vague feeling that had started back in primary school in Ballinrobe from beginning to crystallise: that I didn't entirely belong. That I felt different from most of the other boys. Although in retrospect I know that much of that was down to my sexuality, it was heightened by a school that had a narrow idea of what it meant to be a boy, and an Irish boy in particular.

Irish boys played Gaelic football so we were forced out to play Gaelic football, no matter how much we hated it (rugby and soccer were strictly forbidden, being tainted with Englishness and Protestantism – though somehow tennis was fine), and I would stand around on the side of the pitch, miserable, cold and pissed off, wasting my time, learning absolutely nothing, except how much I hated that stupid game, a hatred I had plenty of time to nurture and care for, standing there in the drizzle.

Irish boys didn't do art. The visual arts were generally suspect and probably foreign, and certainly *smart* Irish boys didn't do art. So I studied art on my own at night and sat the Leaving Cert art exam alone in an empty exam hall.

And Irish boys liked AC/DC, Led Zeppelin and U2 and possibly, at a stretch, Queen (though that Freddie Mercury was a bit weird. He wasn't gay, 'cos he had a moustache and obviously gays didn't have moustaches but, still, there was something queer about him). They definitely didn't listen to The Jacksons, Howard Jones and The Thomson Twins, or jump around singing 'Holiday' by that new girl Madonna.

Boarding school taught me to survive on my own. It also taught me that apparently, like Michael Jackson, I wasn't like other boys.

4. The Big House

I WAS ALWAYS RATHER PROUD of the fact that Ballinrobe had given a word to the English language. It was – and still is – a piece of trivia I wield defensively whenever someone (usually from a dull Dublin suburb) tries to denigrate my generally unremarkable but handsome hometown: 'Has Stillorgan given a word to the English language? No, it bloody hasn't!'

And not just any word either. Not some common-as-muck noun, no fly-by-night adjective, no here-today-gone-tomorrow slang enjoying its brief fifteen minutes in the *Oxford English Dictionary*, but a proper word, an everyday word, a verb, even, and a verb with such weight of meaning that you can't even imagine how the language got along without it before Ballinrobe gave it to the world in 1880.

Seriously, what did people in 1879 say instead of 'boycott'?

Captain Boycott was the unpopular British land agent for an absentee landlord in Ballinrobe, and in 1880 the local people began a campaign of isolation against him, refusing to labour in his fields, serve him in local shops or shoe his horses. When Boycott wrote to *The Times* in London his case became famous and troops were drafted in, but by then a campaign of 'boycotts' had started to spread across the country, and Ballinrobe was already smugly looking down its nose at 'metrosexual' and 'selfie'.

Captain Boycott had lived in Lough Mask House, a large, classic Georgian farmhouse, but by the time Ballinrobe heard the pitter-patter of my ~~tiny~~ large gay feet, the Dalys lived in it. Mr Daly was a client of my dad's, but unlike most of my dad's clients, who eked out precarious livings from Mayo's stony wet soil with a few hardy sheep and resigned-looking cattle, Mr Daly also had a couple of horses and a long driveway. This exotic combination of horses and driveways meant that whenever our father was going on a 'call' to Mr Daly's we would clamour to go with him. Not that it was terribly exciting (after all, my horse-mad middle brother had a sweet but tired old pony called Toffee Apple, who did her best to ignore us in the field beside the house) but 'Mr Daly's' provoked in us a Pavlovian response of giddy excitement.

Ostensibly we wanted to go so we could 'drive' the car. At Mr Daly's gate, my father would stop the car and put you on his knee so you could clutch the steering wheel and 'drive' up the long grass-and-gravel driveway to the big house, while he worked the pedals and jiggled you on his lap and tickled you and pretended to make you crash the car into the ditch, while my sisters screamed in pretend fear in the back seat. But, really, we just wanted to spend time with our dad. A small-town country vet doesn't get days off and on the rare occasions he's at home his small children are often already in bed. So, spending time with our vet dad meant spending time out 'on call' with him in his muddy car that smelt of animals and rain, and rattled and clanked with glass bottles of medicine and scary-looking implements, which were covered with dubious dark stains and the gloopy saliva left behind by muscular cow tongues.

At Mr Daly's I saw a horse being 'covered' for the first time. The mare was standing in the centre of the yard, her ripe horse-womanly pheromones clearly driving the prancing, sex-addled stallion wild, his hoofs clattering on the cobbles till eventually he rather clumsily mounted her, his big bouncing rubbery horse-hose seeming to have a mind of its own as it sought out and found her lady bits, while the men stood around chatting and watching with detached interest. The mare didn't seem to enjoy it much, the stallion was so addled that I doubt he even remembered it, and the men looked as if it fell somewhere between a chore and a local football match. I started out with pretty realistic expectations of sex.

Although the Dalys lived in the infamous captain's

former home, the house, though handsome (a Mayo child's crayon drawing of a farmhouse: a two-storey stone square with a big solid door and five windows), wasn't particularly grand and the Dalys themselves were regular Mayo folk.

But on the other side of the town in Partry House, another of the local 'big houses', Mrs Blosse-Lynch was the real deal: exotically Protestant, imperious and magnificent. The elderly widow of Colonel Blosse-Lynch (or 'Moo', as she called him), she lived in isolated shabby splendour with her lady 'companion', Pat, at the end of her own long driveway, a couple of miles from the town on the edge of a shallow, sandy-bottomed lake. We knew her because on occasion she'd call my father to attend to her friendly dopey Labradors, but most of the town had no reason ever to meet Mrs Blosse-Lynch – but everyone knew her. She would *put-put* into Ballinrobe in her little Citroën 2CV and park with imperious unconcern in the middle of the narrow street outside the grocer's, and until she had collected and packed her shopping into the car, the rest of the town's motorists simply had to wait. And I thought that was fabulous. I already knew a diva when I saw one and Mrs Blosse-Lynch was my first Madonna.

In the hot summer of 1983, after my first year in boarding school, a young American student called Sandra came to stay at Partry House and help harvest the raspberries that Mrs Blosse-Lynch grew in a sizeable plot at the side of the house. Presumably Sandra had come as part of some kind of student 'working abroad' scheme, but it must have been quite an adjustment for an American teenager to find herself living alone with two elderly ladies in the isolated, faded grandeur of Partry House in the West of Ireland in 1983 – a mysterious time, long before Skype and texting, when international telephone calls were so unfathomably costly they were spoken about in hushed tones, and people wrote letters abroad on tissue-thin blue 'airmail' paper to keep the weight down because even letters were an onerous expense.

Not knowing many people in the town, and certainly not knowing any young people, Mrs Blosse-Lynch spoke to my father and soon myself and two of my age-appropriate siblings were drafted in to keep the lonely American company. I didn't need to be drafted: I was eager to sign up. I couldn't wait to see up close how a magnificent Protestant like Mrs Blosse-Lynch lived, and a glossy-haired American (my very own Jaclyn Smith!) was a bonus.

I already had a very high opinion of Protestants. Not only were most of my favourite people Protestants – or at least I assumed Penelope Keith and Felicity Kendal were – but my mother had lived in Protestant England till she was twelve and, even though she was a devout Catholic, we always thought of her as having Protestant bones, which poked through occasionally when she used her 'telephone voice'.

Protestant stuff was just generally better. Even their farms were better. One summer we went to visit our English 'cousins', the Perrys (they weren't actually our cousins but were the family of my mother's childhood best friend) and their farm was amazing. The Mayo mountain farms I went to with my father were hard, mud-worn places, where tough, wiry men picked stones from wet fields and drove wet, suspicious animals into dark shit-splashed sheds. On the Perrys' summer-drenched Pear Tree Farm (I know, they were really rubbing it in with that), there were giant, rolling fields, enormous gleaming harvesting machines, noisy, exhilarating go-karts, huge prickly hay stacks, and crumbly cheese and crusty bread washed down with homemade cider. I felt like Worzel Gummidge. At home, where we were Irish Catholics, we weren't allowed to drive dangerous, petrol-filled go-karts at breakneck speed round scrubby fields, but when we were English Protestants, we could drive *and* drink booze! Being English and Protestant was brilliant. Obviously becoming one of Charlie's Angels was still my first choice but failing that I was going to put down 'Protestant farmer' as my second.

And living the exotic Protestant life at Mrs Blosse-Lynch's was everything I'd hoped. The rheumy-eyed old Labradors wandered distractedly through the house, which, though neat, was showing its age, and the rooms, crowded with the flotsam and jetsam of a storied family life in the big house, were probably a little too much for Mrs Blosse-Lynch and Pat to keep on top of. Not that I cared. To me, the shabby rugs covered with dog hair, and the comfortable threadbare sofas with sun-faded cushions, were talismans of a glorious past, full of shooting parties and pheasants and petticoats and binoculars and charming people saying charming things over fancy dishes. But the glassy eyes of the dusty animal heads that hung on the walls didn't just look down on a disappeared past, they looked down on a present where the past still shimmered through, like an image from my father's old cine projector. Once, while taking off her wellington boots by the stairs, Mrs Blosse-Lynch saw me examining a small, carved wooden box. 'It's from India,' she said casually, and I wondered would she have said, 'It's from Mars,' just as casually, because to me they were pretty much the same thing.

There was a lawn tennis court, and even though it hadn't been tended in years it was still usable, and we would play tennis or croquet while Mrs Blosse-Lynch watched and Pat brought out cucumber sandwiches (actual cucumber sandwiches), which we thought were hilarious and disgusting till we ate them and found out they were crunchy and delicious.

Years later the fully fledged gay version of me looked back and, based on no evidence whatsoever, fantasised that Mrs Blosse-Lynch and Pat were lesbian lovers; pioneering, no-nonsense, tweed-skirted, wellington-wearing lesbians, who'd make each other boiled eggs and listen to the wireless together on their arse-worn sofas while shaggy Labradors snored on their faded lesbian rugs. I thought this was a wonderful idea, but when I mentioned it to my mother she rolled her eyes and did that 'Rory!' thing she does when she thinks I'm being ridiculous. And when I mentioned to her that I was writing about Mrs Blosse-Lynch, she said, 'Oh, please don't put in about you wanting them to be lesbians! You'll upset someone.' But it shouldn't. I wanted them to be lesbians for me. I wanted to come from a town where lesbians lived in ramshackle houses with dozy old dogs, because that town would have felt more like home to an older me.

There was a dilapidated boathouse at the bottom of the garden on the lake shore, and we would push out the big old row-boat and row through the reeds, then swim in the clear water and dive down to push our hands into the soft sandy bottom (all the other lakes around had dark bog water and rocky bottoms – even Protestant lakes were better!). We'd dry off in the sun, asking Sandra about America and giggling because we found out that Mrs Blosse-Lynch's name was actually Lois, which my sister Edel would repeat in a posh accent. My red-haired and Irish-freckled brother Fergal fancied Sandra, with her American hair and tanned American skin, and he kissed her. They had a summer romance and we all wished she would come back every year so we could play croquet and eat cucumber sandwiches and hold boxes from India.

We were only a couple of miles from our own house, yet we were in another world. A world that reminded me of the worlds I had already discovered between the pages of books or on Saturday-afternoon TV with the curtains drawn. In Partry House I was one of *The Famous Five* or *Little Lord Fauntleroy* or Mary in *The Secret Garden*. And I was already beginning to realise that I liked other worlds, because other worlds didn't care if I liked football and other worlds didn't care if I went to mass. Mrs Blosse-Lynch didn't care if I went to mass – she didn't care if the whole town was sitting in their cars waiting for her to pick up her groceries!

5. Finding Homo

I HAD NO IDEA WHAT I wanted to do with my life when I finished school. I didn't yet know who I was so how could I possibly know who I wanted to be? I knew what I *didn't* want to be: I didn't want to be boring. And at sixteen, as far as I was concerned, everything was boring. Ballinrobe was boring, school was boring, exams were boring, football was boring, mass was boring ... Everything was just so *boring*. I would lie in bed refusing to get up in a vain attempt to stave off the inevitable onset of another day of inevitable boringness. I had taken to my bed like a Victorian lady with the malaise, and the only thing that got me out of it was Pierce Brosnan and Stephanie Zimbalist in *Remington Steele*.

I, of course, was the smart and sassy Stephanie, my jacket sleeves pushed up to three-quarter length, exasperated by, and secretly in love with, the suave and handsome Pierce, whom I hired to be the face of my detective agency because the sexist 1980s wouldn't take seriously a cute, sassy lady private detective. I would have put down 'Smart and Sassy Lady Private Detective Teamed Up with Pierce Brosnan' on my CAO form if it had been an option but unfortunately, and ridiculously, it was not a course offered by any of the recognised colleges.

I did know a couple of things, though.

I knew I was interested in art – or, at least, I knew it didn't bore me and that was roughly the same thing. I spent most of my waking hours doodling on everything within reach, much to the exasperation of everyone who owned anything within reach. Books, desks, newspapers, magazines, tablecloths, walls – everything slowly became engulfed in a tide of cartoon doodles of glamorous women with evening gloves and nipped waists, lantern-jawed men, fat opera singers, goofy dogs, majestic horses and futuristic cars.

And I knew I wanted to find other queers. By that point I knew *technically* that gays existed – I'd read about them, I'd heard about them, I'd seen them on the telly – but, rather like my then increasingly tenuous belief in God, I believed in gays only as a matter of faith. I'd been told they existed so I had to accept that they did, but I still hadn't met a real-live, fully paid-up, card-carrying gay, and I was beginning to worry that if I didn't meet one soon I'd become a gaytheist. I needed proof.

So I applied to art college.

It was a very small one on the edge of Dublin in Dún Laoghaire with only a couple of hundred students, and on my very first day I sat in the queue for registration beside an impossibly handsome bleach-blond Mohawked punk, who was wearing a pair of pyjamas with a *Playboy* centrefold safety-pinned to the back. He was so beautiful and so exciting I couldn't bring myself to look directly at him, terrified that if I did I might not be able to stop myself throwing myself onto his lap and kissing him full on the mouth.

But my small art college turned out not to be the homo-filled, gender-bendin' 1986 gaytopia I'd hoped for. In fact, there turned out to be only one other definitely queer student. Handsome, brown-eyed, exotically coiffed and dressed like a *Face* magazine cover, Niall was universally thought of as one of the school's most talented students, so he was a good one to have onboard but, still, he was the only one. And Niall was a year ahead of me so even though we would eventually become close friends and lifelong collaborators, that first year it was up to me to find queers on my own.

In the Dublin of 1986, still seven years before homosexual acts were decriminalised, just finding other gays was a job worthy of Jessica Fletcher. Today, with two clicks of a cursor, gay kids can be chatting to other gay kids or watching the badly lit homemade pornography of an exhibitionist French couple and their horny friend Pascale. And if they have the right app on their phone, they can tell you how many metres they are from the nearest Dominant Verbal Top, who likes holding hands and nights in on the sofa with a glass of wine and a movie. And everyone knows where the brightly lit, rainbow-flag-flying gay bars are. The world and their granny can tell you where The George is and chances are Granny has already been there one Sunday to see Shirley Temple Bar's *Bingo* show.

But in 1986, on Saturday afternoons, I would take the 46A bus into the city centre on my mission to find the gays, these creatures of myth and legend and crude schoolyard jokes. I was still a country boy, and the city was still exciting and full of possibilities to me. I was blind to the crumbling plasterwork, peeling fly posters and boarded-up shop fronts of depressed eighties Dublin, and all I saw were interesting people hurrying to interesting assignations. I would wander the streets, soaking up everything and everyone, and fumble with the change in my pocket, separating out the return bus fare and counting what was left.

Every now and then I'd see that elusive creature who made my pulse quicken a little: another gay. I couldn't always be totally sure – my gaydar was still underdeveloped, and the New Romantics were muddying the waters at the time – but sometimes I'd get a glancing eye contact that confirmed my teenage suspicions. I would go to Marx Bros café, which was popular with punks and cycle couriers and, it was rumoured, with 'the gays'. I'd buy coffee from the shaven-headed server (was he a gay?) and sit nervously at a table, cautiously eyeing the clientele for signs of gayness, signs of me. I'd buy *Hot Press* magazine, and in the back there were small ads where farmers were looking for farmers, and nice 'regular' blokes from the midlands were looking for other nice regular blokes who could travel.

And there was always an ad for 'Ice Breakers', a monthly meeting of a gay youth group where nervous and skittish new gays could meet other nervous and skittish new gays over cups of tea in a room at the Clarence Hotel and be nervous and skittish together under the watchful eye of an experienced proper gay. Nowadays, of course, the Clarence is fancy and U2-owned, but in 1986 it smelt of polish and served roast dinners to country priests who were up in Dublin to see the bishop. So, on the first Thursday of the month, I found myself sitting in a circle of hotel chairs announcing to strangers that I was gay, while in the room next door a circle of strangers announced to each other that they were alcoholics.

I've never been one for chair circles or groups so I sipped my tea and dunked my biscuit and felt uncomfortable throughout, but I had definitely, without doubt, *finally* found some other gays. Only a small handful of nervous gays but that was enough – they were my gay slippery slope, the thin edge of the homo wedge – and after the tea and biscuits the two guys who had led the meeting brought us to a gay club and that was all I needed. Here were the gays! And lots of them.

All along the gays had been hiding right under my nose but I just hadn't known where to look. How many times had I passed this club, Hooray Henry's, tucked into the corner of the Powerscourt Townhouse Centre, not knowing that at night it was full of exuberant, drunk gays with faded denims, frosted tips and Hi-NRG 12 inches?

And that night, while Hazell Dean continued 'Searchin' (Lookin' For Love)', an older hairdresser with bleached hair gave up the search and settled on awkward sex with me.

Pre-decriminalisation, Irish gays existed in a shadowy twilight world of their own devising. The laws that criminalised sex between men weren't generally enforced – there weren't gangs of gardaí sweeping through Bewley's on a Saturday afternoon throwing queens and half-finished éclairs into police vans – but the legal and social uncertainty pushed the gay community underground, after dark and behind closed doors.

Today the lines between the gay and straight worlds have blurred. Their edges have bled into each other. Gok Wan is in your mother's living room, hen parties are in the local gay bar, rainbow-flag-draped leather queens shimmy down O'Connell Street every June and, according to the internet, Pat Butcher is going out with Hyacinth Bouquet.

But in the Dublin of 1986, becoming an *actively gay* gay, a proper cast-iron gay, a sexually active gay with purposeful erections and Grace Jones, you had to turn your back on the heterosexual daytime world you'd known until now and agree to enter a new underground gay world, which somehow managed to exist hidden in plain sight of the everyday world that surrounded it – an everyday world that suddenly seemed to me to be dull and dreary and grey. Like Harry Potter's first letter from Hogwarts, that night in Hooray Henry's revealed to me a previously secret world. I was wide-eyed Harry Poofter, discovering the hidden magical world of Witchcraft and Faggotry, while only feet away the straight muggles caught the night bus home to their grey muggle lives, unaware that in the basements below their feet the gays were building a new world out of disco and poppers.

And I *loved* it.

My underground den of iniquity of choice was Minsky's. I would spend the evening with my art-school flatmates in Dún Laoghaire, then catch the last bus into town, nervous, excited, taut like a bow string. Tucked off salubrious St Stephen's Green, Minsky's was the ground floor and basement of a large Georgian townhouse in an imposing terrace that had long ago been converted into the offices of dentists and accountants. Up the steps and behind the large Georgian door, a riotous queen in a makeshift cloakroom under the grand staircase would take your money and your coat, before you were ushered through to the ground-floor bar with a wave of a decidedly unashamed, defiantly limp wrist. Inside was a rather grand Georgian parlour with moulded ceilings, expensively upholstered furniture, side tables, carpet and gilt frames, while two leather queens and Anne Doyle propped up the bar. Gays of every hue stood around chatting and good-naturedly slagging each other, checking out the new arrivals while drinking glasses of wine or Campari and orange.

Not a beer or a spirit in sight: before the licensing laws were changed in the early nineties, Dublin's nightclubs were technically 'restaurants'. That meant that in order to stay within the law, late-night drinking and dancing establishments had to serve food – which usually meant that at one a.m. a desultory (and possibly dangerous) chicken curry would be brought out, or a few baskets of chips and cocktail sausages passed around. It also meant that they could serve only wine – so even the butchest, moustachioed, denim and plaid-covered 'clone' would be daintily sipping a nice sweet Riesling or a dry sherry.

But the real action was downstairs.

A narrow staircase led to a small, dark basement where swirling lights, mirrors and a hard-working smoke machine made a compact, loud dance floor seem bigger than it was. And on that dance floor men would be *dancing*. And I mean *proper* dancing. Feeling the rhythm, the beat, the emotional arc of the music and allowing their bodies to move in response to it. You know ... actual *dancing*.

In 1986, straight Irish men didn't dance. Oh, sure, at weddings the men would eventually be so polluted drunk that they'd stumble and flail around to 'Eye Of The Tiger'. And, yes, teenage boys with bird's-nest hair would close their eyes and nod their heads to The Cure, and working-class boys with denim jackets would tap cigarette ash and jerk a foot in time to Thin Lizzy, but they didn't actually dance. Before the arrival of ecstasy and dance music, straight Irish guys didn't dance for fear of looking gay. Expressing yourself in any way was considered suspect and gay, and even the only two legitimate forms of artistic expression allowed to straight men – writing and acting – were allowed only if combined with a prodigious drink problem and syphilis. But in Minsky's the men danced. They twirled and slid and shuffled and swayed and dipped and shimmied and popped and got down. They spread their arms and spun each other, clapped and did silly synchronised moves, laughed and whooped and rushed onto the floor to demand 'How Will I Know' by that gorgeous Whitney Houston girl.

And in Minsky's it was perfectly OK to like that song by the sweet, fresh-faced Whitney Houston. Outside it was not OK to like Whitney Houston. Outside, Irish muggle boys were only allowed to like U2 and Hothouse Flowers and AC/DC and Madness, and maybe a *little* David Bowie because he got a pass on the gay stuff because of all the drugs but, still, you can't like Bowie too much 'cos it'd be poncy. While the rest of Europe was embracing synthesisers and New Romantics and makeup and big hair and Bronski Beat and even Madonna, Dublin remained suspicious of all that. Oh, sure, there were pockets of New Romantics hanging around town, but for the most part Dublin remained stubbornly a hippie rock town where music journalists had long curly hair and testicles. But behind the Georgian door of Minsky's (and the handful of other gay clubs) we didn't give a crap about U2 or Status Quo. Rock music represented everything that excluded us. Every uncomfortable teenage disco. Every suspicion that I wasn't 'regular' enough, every uncomfortable silence when I'd been asked if I'd seen 'the match' last night. On the dance floor of Minsky's we danced and sweated and took poppers to 'Diana', Eurythmics, Ashford & Simpson, Frankie Goes To Hollywood, Kool & The Gang, Chaka Khan, Deniece Williams, and Pointer Sisters special imports.

There was sex, too, of course. If you weren't dancing you were cruising – leaning oh-so-casually against the wall, cradling your tepid glass, your eyes smarting from cigarette smoke and Giorgio For Men, scanning the room with studied nonchalance, rigorously avoiding eye contact with the creepy old fella to the left (you didn't want to encourage him) while hoping (in vain) that the hot dark-haired guy in the white denim jacket, who, someone once told you, was a 'part-time' model, might notice you and give you the return glance that let you know you were in with a shot. If you were lucky you might catch the eye of some guy with a moustache and a bedsit on the South Circular Road, but even if he lived at home with his mammy or his wife you could always go to the ladies' toilet for a quick fumble and a clumsy snog. There wasn't much call for a ladies' toilet in Minsky's so an enterprising queen had usually removed the light bulb.

Past the toilets was the door out to a back laneway, which, in those days before the smoking ban, was used in the summer months for cruising and making out – to everyone's mischievous delight, because the lane was overlooked by the offices of Opus Dei.

Excitingly, here in the gay demi-monde, all the things that marked me out as weird or different in the regular straight world didn't matter at all. In fact, everything that was 'wrong' about me out there wasn't just OK here in Minsky's, it was 'right' – it just made me an even better gay. Knowing all the words to 'Wham! Rap' didn't make me a poncy faggot, it made me a fun faggot! Having a strong opinion on the Madonna vs Cyndi Lauper debate wasn't suspiciously gay, it was *de rigueur*. (The gays even used French in casual conversation!) No one in Minsky's was ever going to ask me whether I'd seen the match last night, and if they did I'd have gone looking for Derry the owner to tell him I thought maybe one of the Opus Dei people was in on a spying mission. Of course the gays had – and still have – their own hang-ups about masculinity, but they mostly concern whether or not they want to sleep with you or introduce you to their parents, and on the dance floor at Minsky's I was free to be me without fear or favour.

The community I had discovered under the mirrorball was a much more democratic society than the daytime world outside. Or, at least, the hierarchies the gays had developed were entirely different from those outside. They were custom-made – of the gays, by the gays, for the gays, one 'gaytion' under Olivia Newton-John. Outside, people were socially sorted by seemingly random attributes. Being good at sports, especially field sports, conferred sometimes stratospheric status on men in the regular world, even though it seemed unlikely that an ability to play football well was ever going to save a baby from a burning skyscraper. Owning particular kinds of cars was respected. I am always terrified that one day I will witness a horrible crime and see the perpetrator drive off in the getaway car. When the police ask me what kind of car it was, all I'll be able to mumble is that it was the same colour as those cute shorts I got in Sitges three years ago. In the heterosexual world, on the other side of Minsky's Georgian door, being Bono was something, whereas on the homosexual side of Minsky's door the only member of U2 who even came *close* to mattering was Larry, the hot one.

Being hot counted for a lot. If you were hot, no one cared whether you drove a Ferrari or cycled a bicycle – a

Ferrari wasn't going to fuck you all night long, then ask you for its bus fare home in the morning. The scene had its hot stars – the sexy moustachioed 'clone' or the snake-hipped blond 'twink' – but all gay life was represented and the democracy of hotness, combined with the small scene, meant that the social demarcations that existed outside were blurred or erased altogether. Barristers hung out with electricians, who dated professors, who fucked taxi drivers, who had affairs with rent boys, who lent money to students, who woke up with an architect, who caught his farmer in the ladies' toilet with that solicitor who once helped him out for free when he had that bother with the TV licence when he was a poor student. That social free-for-all is one of the great joys of a gay scene. Walk into any straight bar in any city and the patrons will all be roughly the same: roughly the same age, roughly the same social background, with roughly the same accent and roughly the same interests. In a gay bar, Darndale and Dalkey are chewing the face off each other and you can get legal advice or a plumber in the ladies' toilet.

I met Gerry and Dennis in Minsky's. They were a handsome couple, Gerry a TV writer and Dennis an architect, and I fancied both of them. They were good to me, and we would drive out to the edge of the city to see the motorways being built – I thought it was the height of sophistication. Gerry wrote for the hottest show on TV at the time. *Nighthawks* was ground-breaking and hugely popular, part chat show, part soap opera, part sketch show, and when I first started doing drag, Gerry wrote a series of sketches about Sean the Transvestite Farmer. I would get into drag in the RTÉ studios and then we would drive out to a large farm near Maynooth.

We didn't want to spook the farmer who owned the place so we would film on days when he was at the mart. Only his confused-looking sons would be there when we spilled out of the car to film in sequins and blond curls. The sketches involved me prancing through fields of sheep lip-syncing to Dusty Springfield's 'You Don't Have To Say You Love Me' in gold lamé, or strolling through giant sheds full of thousands of gobble-gobbling turkeys with a wistful look in my eye, or polishing the exhaust of my tractor in gold wellington boots, while a voiceover (by the recognisable voice of RTÉ's then agricultural reporter) would dully intone about the effects of European agricultural policy on farmers like Sean. They weren't ever going to win any comedy awards but they were good, stupid fun.

Years later, when I returned to Dublin from Japan in the mid-nineties, one of the first things I did was attend Gerry's funeral. It was a nice day and a fitting service for a fun, kind, smart guy like Gerry, but his timing was terrible. Gerry was one of the last people I knew who died before HIV treatments started to improve.

6. Making a Show of Myself

BACK IN ART SCHOOL I drew and painted and printed, but mostly I just hung out. I lived with friends in grim, mouldy basement flats and drank cheap booze, and when I had to, I made mediocre work. In the summers I would go to France, work on a maize farm (where I had sex in a tent with a girl for the first time, a loud and determined older girl from Leeds, while my friend Liam had sex with her friend in the tent next door) and sell ice creams on the beach.

My straight college friends were art students and therefore thrilled to have a gay friend until they remembered how annoying I was. Occasionally they would come with me to Minsky's, enjoying their dips into this cologne-drenched gay secret society. And I became good friends with Niall, the school's other gay, who, it turned out, had an older boyfriend who managed an arty gay nightclub in town called Sides.

Sides was the difference between a 'niteclub' and *clubbing*. Whereas Minsky's was the gay cousin of Dublin's Leeson Street establishments – local, fun, boozy, upholstered, the Nolan Sisters – Sides was clubbing in the new mould: house music, strobe lights, big sound system, stripped-back dance floor and new drugs, the descendant of Studio 54 and The Blitz. Niall would spend endless hours designing and making intricate fliers for glitter and staple-gun parties like the 'Andy Warhol Obituary Party' where our friend Wendy did cookery demonstrations that involved shoving things into a microwave and seeing if they exploded. People dressed up – they made costumes and poured paint on themselves, boys wore makeup and put glue in their hair, and one night there was a silly drag party called the Alternative Miss Ireland. It helped to be beautiful at Sides (it helps to be beautiful everywhere) but at Sides for the first time I saw that people could also *make* themselves beautiful. And if they couldn't quite achieve beauty, well, they could certainly achieve *interesting* –

'I like your hair.'

'Thanks. I made it out of flour and Monster Munch.'

'You lost a bit at the back.'

'I know. A seagull grabbed it when I got off the bus.'

After my first year in art school I had decided to eschew fine art for design, and I enjoyed it, even though my work was generally pedestrian. However, by the time I finished my third year, with only one more to go, I realised I didn't want to be a graphic designer. In fact, the thought of spending the rest of my life at a drawing table, illustrating cereal boxes for men in suits, filled me with dread. But I had to do just one more year and then I'd at least have my piece of paper to show for my time there. Something for my parents. Now I had to decide what I would do with that final year. What big project would I spend the year working on that would be assessed and judged, and would decide whether or not I was an art-school graduate or an art-school failure? I had no idea but I had the whole summer to think about it.

Before Ryanair came along the only people who flew off this island were expensive racehorses and landed gentry with monocles so, like everyone else, I took the ferry, then the train, and turned up in Chelsea to stay with my older brother Lorcan, who at the time worked for a famous and moneyed contemporary art gallery.

That first night Lorcan threw a party. In the kitchen I came across a large, imposing Australian, who was wearing a ridiculous wig and a tweed jacket that appeared to have tiny swastikas embroidered all over it. He was holding forth loudly in a good-humoured argument over his sartorial choices, defending the offending jacket on the basis that the swastika was, after all, a Hindu symbol meaning 'wellbeing' and other people's ignorance was none of his business.

That was Leigh Bowery. As an art student in the 1980s, I was already aware of Leigh Bowery. He was a club legend and performance artist, who had made a name for himself as a living work of art, a Clubland flesh-and-blood sculpture, a towering voluptuous installation of skin and costume that moved with surprising grace through crowded rooms of startled clubbers or puzzled gallery patrons. His astonishing costumes, which seemed to push his very human flesh into impossible, unsettling, inhuman shapes, set a standard for which every club kid with ping-pong balls stuck to his face has been striving ever since.

For Leigh, his body wasn't an end, it was a beginning; a medium of transformation, an opportunity. With paint and fabric, movement and performance, he pushed against the boundaries of his own form, his own biology – and *transformed* himself.

In Leigh I began to see all sorts of new possibilities. He was a doughy kid from a tiny town in the asshole of Australia, yet here he was, the startling epicentre of cool London, the most fabulous creature in a scene full of fabulous creatures where what you decided to be was more important than who you were expected to be.1 For the first time in my life I realised that I didn't have to be defined by Ballinrobe, County Mayo: I could define *myself*. I was the master of my own destiny! Life was for creating, not consuming! Convention was for wimps! And being gay, far from being a burden or a limitation, was a *gift* because it freed me from a wearying weight of expectation. I was queer Rory and there was no

---

[1] Sadly, Leigh died of an AIDS-related illness, in 1994, aged 33.

character arc for queer Rory. Queers weren't expected to settle down with a nice woman, we weren't expected to get steady, reliable jobs and raise steady, reliable kids. I wasn't expected to be anyone's godfather in case I burst into flames or to join the local Tidy Towns committee or volunteer to steward at the Community Games because I'd only make everyone else uncomfortable.

All that was expected of me was to look nice and not kill anyone.

For the rest of the summer I would turn up at gay clubs, wide-eyed with the possibilities, and this huge, magnificent creature would greet me with a squeal and encourage me to get into as much trouble as possible. The next morning, after dancing all night, kissing boys and ending up on the night bus, I'd turn up tired but grinning to my summer job as a waiter in a small fish restaurant on Drury Lane.

The manager there was an outrageous English queen with long black hair that hung in a flatiron ponytail down his back. He had an encyclopaedic knowledge and perfect recall of classic camp movies. On quiet days and between servings he would entertain me (and himself) by acting out the plot and best scenes from his favourites. One day I might be working with Elizabeth Taylor in *Suddenly Last Summer*, shrieking, 'They devoured him!' or polishing spoons with Joan Crawford in *Johnny Guitar*, and the next I'm trying to set tables and keep up with the barbed remarks of *The Women*. Later, when I saw these movies, I'd often be disappointed because they had been so much better in his telling.

Once a year he and his boyfriend would drag up to go to an annual party. Months beforehand the photo album of previous years was taken out and pored over before the movie reference was chosen for that year's production. For weeks beforehand the costumes were being made, the accessories sorted and the makeup perfected, and for one night my fun, sweet restaurant manager was whatever immaculate and perfect screen goddess he wanted to be. It turned out that you could be from Croydon and still be Barbara Stanwyck.

All that summer of 1989, at the end of the restaurant's street, the Theatre Royal Drury Lane was a hive of activity as they prepared to open a brand new musical that autumn called *Miss Saigon*. Cast and crew would come in, and much of the talk was about technical difficulties they were having with a helicopter that was supposed to land spectacularly onstage during the show. And when the show finally opened the street was cordoned off and we closed the restaurant so we could stand behind the barriers and wait to see Princess Diana arrive. And when she stepped out of the car and waved, bird thin in diaphanous pale blue, the burst of camera flash was so intense and so bright the whole world was momentarily overexposed.

That summer of fun changed everything for me, and when I stumbled back to Dublin, tired and gayer than ever, I was absolutely sure I didn't want to be a graphic designer. It wouldn't be fair on me *or* design. Instead, I was on a mission to find a new, more fabulous me and I would leave no sequin unturned – but I still had to get through that final year of college *and* I had to do it without being bored to death. So, after thinking about it for all of ten minutes, I decided to spend my final year designing a drag show. At first that didn't go down too well with my college tutors, but after I'd assured them that I would include enough traditional design elements to pass muster (posters, set, costume, illustration ...), they allowed it. I think they already knew I'd be no great loss to the design community.

So, while my classmates did real work and prepared for careers as designers, I spent the time smoking cigarettes and trying to make a gown out of chicken wire and Copydex. I knew nothing about drag, nothing about making costumes, and nothing about making shows, but none of that stopped me. I *had* made plenty of puppets since I was a kid (and had even made student cash doing my own version of a *Punch and Judy* show at Christmas parties in factories) and figured a drag show couldn't be that much different. I'd never even seen a traditional drag show, but I had the entirely misplaced confidence of youth and the couldn't-give-a-fuck freedom that came from already knowing I was unemployable.

I wrote a basic script for a fictional show starring a fictional queen called Simply Devune – a name I'd taken from a ridiculously camp movie called *Will Success Spoil Rock Hunter?* starring Jayne Mansfield, during which the pneumatic Jayne would squeakily exclaim that everything was 'simply devune!' I drew sets and lighting plans, took photographs, and did line drawings that would be projected onto screens during this fictional show. I designed posters and tickets, then screen-printed them by hand. I made a ridiculous, uncomfortable and impractical dress, which I covered with surgical gloves and sprayed gold. The paint I used reacted with the rubber in the gloves and never quite dried so the dress would stick to everything it touched and leave a gold residue behind, as if a glamorous slug had passed clumsily by. And in those pre-eBay shopping days, I made matching ugly man-sized mules.

The show was awful on paper, but I was young and fun and stupid (and possibly a little high) so that didn't seem like any reason not to put it on. After all, I decided, it was silly to go to all that bother and *not* put it on. And so it came about that I mounted the show for all the students in the college and for the external assessors from the Department of Education.

I persuaded my indulgent straight friends to be in it. I had two of my girlfriends dressed as purple furry angels on swings (I don't remember why) and two fit game-for-a-laugh straight boys topless and baby-oiled (I don't need to remember why). Neither do I remember what the show was supposed to be about, if anything, but I stole jokes from old songs and, with arty student pretensions, I started the show sitting at a table as a boy and slowly applied terrible makeup. On their way in, each audience member had been given an inflated plastic vet's 'arm glove' – the kind vets use to shove their hands up cows' arses – to wave pointlessly. I'm pretty sure there was absolutely no rhyme or reason to that except I thought it would be funny and stupid, and it was definitely one of those (and possibly both). My sister came and sat near the front, wondering what on earth art school had done to her tow-headed little brother, and the Department of Education assessors were clearly so confused and traumatised that they lost their reason because they gave me my piece of paper.

I was twenty years old, an art-school graduate, and an absolute fucking chancer.

7. Setting Out

AFTER MY ART-SCHOOL SHOW, Niall's boyfriend, Frank, decided to let me do a show in Sides. Actually, 'let me do a show' gives the wrong impression. As was to be the case very often over the years, essentially Frank (and later Niall) had a nutty idea for a show and, unlike every other right-thinking person, I didn't say, 'Fuck off, Frank, I'm not doing that!' In a pattern that would reach its apogee years later, when I was giving myself paint enemas to the delighted horror of clubbers in a dodgy club in the Docklands, Niall and Frank would come up with a complicated idea for a ridiculous show that nobody in their right mind (including Frank and Niall) would actually do – except me. I was the best fully poseable doll ever.

And so one Saturday night I found myself doing my first 'professional' drag gig, lip-syncing to Klaus Nomi songs and emerging from a tube of stretch fabric, like a drunk, gay sausage roll with a pointy cardboard headpiece and a crappy wig, in front of a room of utterly unimpressed gays and increasingly angry lesbians. Frank watched from behind his fingers, Niall thought it was hilarious, and I wanted to die. It was *fabulous*!

But grey, depressed 1989 Dublin was a difficult place to be fabulous and, like most other young Irish people of the time, I was almost expected to leave. London was the obvious choice, but then my friend Helen and I read a book by the travel writer Paul Theroux called *Riding the Iron Rooster* about train journeys through Communist China, and suddenly London seemed like a boring idea. Instead, just months after the Tiananmen Square massacre, and just weeks after the Berlin Wall had come down, we set off by train with our waiter's tips and a vague plan: try to get into Soviet Russia, somehow find black market tickets for the Trans-Siberian Express, get across Mongolia, through China, and eventually take a boat to Japan where we imagined we could get jobs teaching English. And all this we figured we would just *do*, without visas or (in those pre-internet days) any real information. All we had was the fearlessness and ignorance of youth and a vague rumour we had heard from a friend of a friend of a bloke we'd met in a pub once: a nameless professor at a university in Budapest might help if we could find him.

The weird thing was, I didn't even like Asian food at the time. In truth, the whole thing was Helen's idea. *Stands up and points wildly at Helen*. She was, and still is, a kind of post-hippie adventurer. (I used to call her and her sister 'The Bamboo and Snot Sisters' because they would make everything they needed, from clothes to camera bags, out of whatever seemed to be to hand, and I always imagined they'd be very handy if you ever found yourself trapped on a desert island with them. You'd soon be living in tropical splendour in a quirky treehouse with a system of slides and pulleys made from bamboo and snot.) Helen decided this would be a great, why-the-hell-not, possibly-achievable adventure – she just needed someone to go with her. And I, as we already know, am easily led. I was also bored, and being bored was the thing I feared most, and this stupid idea didn't sound *entirely* boring (except possibly for all the parts where we spent weeks on end in trains) and so I thought, OK, let's do that instead.

The story I am trying (in my own way) to tell you here is *not* the story of how two kids, with nothing but a pocketful of dreams, recurring conjunctivitis and a lot of blind good luck (in particular, our timing was excellent – the Soviet Union was crumbling and everyone had more to worry about than two Irish kids with home haircuts and no tickets), spent half of 1990 travelling painfully slowly overland from Dublin to Tokyo. So apart from mentioning that I was briefly arrested for trading in endangered animals (or something – obviously I was entirely innocent, and I didn't speak Mongolian), and a skinny, bespectacled, middle-aged man dressed *Starsky & Hutch*-style pressed his erection into my thigh on a bus in Shanghai – how the hell did Chinese Starsky even know I was gay? – I'll move the narrative on:

We arrived in Tokyo.

8. Japanti

WE ARRIVED WITH NO EXPECTATIONS, less money and not a single word of Japanese (beyond the shaky ability to count to ten we'd learned on the boat from Shanghai). It was like walking into a world specifically designed to be entirely alien. We had left behind a provincial, recession-battered country that looked determinedly backwards, where the Pope's visit in 1979 was still regarded as some kind of national high point, where a young person's ambition extended no further than the ferry to London, where sex between men was a criminal offence, divorce was unavailable, the sale of condoms required a doctor's prescription, you couldn't buy a beer in a nightclub, pregnant girls went away for a few months and came back without babies and priests could be famous just for being priests. And suddenly we were standing in the centre of a gleaming, futuristic, forward-looking, cash-rich, crowded, humid megalopolis with moving pavements, where the toilets wiped your ass for you, department stores sold single, huge polished apples in fancy presentation boxes, and we had absolutely no responsibilities and only one aim: *to have a good time.*

We found a single room in a *gaijin* house (a 'foreigner' house) with five or six other young foreigners, all of whom were teaching English or hoping to. A creaking, traditional Japanese building with an outside toilet, it was squeezed precariously between newer ones on a commercial street. Our room, like the others, had a tiny sink, a single gas ring, a wardrobe, traditional *tatami*-mat flooring and, like a tired sitcom gag, a window that faced onto the neighbouring wall inches away. There was no air-conditioning and, in the intense summer humidity, I would soak a sheet in the tiny sink and sit on the floor wrapped in it, like a wet ghost.

I found a job fairly quickly, teaching English for a large chain of schools through which I managed to wangle a work visa, but Helen had trouble: getting a visa was more complicated if you weren't a graduate, and she had dropped out of college. Eventually she took a job in a small town in the countryside and became my visiting country cousin for a year before she became a student herself, returned to Tokyo, and we moved into a decent apartment with our own toilet and air-conditioning.

The chain of English-language schools I worked for was a weird, vaguely cultish enterprise called Bi-

Lingual, owned by Ms Minami, a middle-aged Japanese woman who styled herself as a cross between Kate Bush and a Victorian doll. Ms Minami was well known in Japan, where successful businesswomen were a novelty, and she affected a public image of soft-focus girlish eccentricity. Her bizarre Baby Jane aesthetic was half-heartedly translated into the schools, which, although mostly situated in business districts beside railway stations or in nondescript office buildings, were all candy-striped wallpaper, lace trimmings, pink plastic tables and reproduction 'period' furniture. Even the school's logo was a giant pink bow. It was a school designed by a child who'd eaten too much candyfloss at Disneyland.

But boring stuff, like work and visas (and food and sleep), was just an annoying distraction from my deadly serious mission to have fun. I quickly discovered and made a second home of Tokyo's infamous gay district, Ni-chōme, a small warren of narrow streets crammed with tiny bars, a couple of which catered specifically to foreigners and the Japanese guys who liked them. For the first (but not the last) time in my life I was a fetish! I fell home drunk every morning and fell in love every night. I hoovered up dark-eyed, soft-lipped Japanese boys and marvelled at their spiky pubic hair. I climbed into bed with Korean waiters and woke up on futons with Israeli dancers, Canadian writers and a French hairdresser. A handsome big-dicked photographer took me back to his stylish apartment and, to my mortification, during the night I drunkenly pissed his bed. I was young, fun and hungry for life, running around with my tongue out, like a puppy in a ball pen.

The Japanese have a very relaxed, uncomplicated attitude to sex – including gay sex – unencumbered by prudery or guilt. However, social conventions are very strong and 'alternative' lifestyles are frowned upon, so, while gay sex might not be a big deal in itself, living a gay life and rejecting the expected path of a steady job with a wife and two kids is a very big deal indeed. So, although the denizens of Ni-chōme were generally looked upon with a kind of indulgent amusement, they were, nevertheless, considered misfits, which tended to attract kindred spirits.

New Sazae was a small, dingy, one-room bar, bathed in the red glow of coloured light-bulbs up a flight of narrow stairs on the second floor of a small grey building. It wasn't a gay bar so much as a *misfit* bar, whose clientele of punks, gangsters, artists, junkies, transvestites, nuts, prostitutes and runaways felt comfortable among its tatty stools and graffiti-scrawled walls, tucked away among the gays of Ni-chōme. It soon became my regular haunt for drinking bottles of beer and learning slang from ageing hair-oiled gangsters or making a fool of myself over some pretty tattooed rock-a-billy with a bored girlfriend. And overseeing this collection of friendly weirdoes and interesting oddballs was a sweet, skinny, older leather queen, who knew everyone by name and treated everyone, whether prostitute or businessman, with the same easy maternal familiarity.

It was here, among the beer and the drugs and the stories, that I found a family of sorts. Tall, handsome, floppy-haired misfit Masa showed me how to make Japanese food and eventually ended up marrying my friend Sandy, a blonde English girl from the *gaijin* house. Crinkle-eyed, shuffling, long-haired misfit Kazua was never without his camera and always smiley-stoned. And sweet, funny misfit Hiroko, with her fringe always in her eyes, was already considered a dubious spinster in her late twenties. We'd stay up all night dancing and taking speed, then she'd potter off to her dull office job where her shamelessly unconventional lifestyle was cause for suspicion and gossip. Hiroko refused to bend to other people's expectations.

There are, however, no expectations to bend to if you're a gay twenty-two-year-old foreigner in Tokyo. I was free to be whomever and *whatever* I wanted to be. And it turned out that what I wanted to be was Panti.

In the spring of 1992 I met Angelo in a well-known bar popular with foreigners. A compact, doe-eyed Italian-American from Atlanta, he was on his first visit to Ni-chōme, having only recently arrived in Japan, and we became friends immediately, bonding over a shared sense of humour and similar taste in movies and fellas. It also turned out we had a shared interest in drag.

Angelo was a much more experienced queen than I. He had started doing drag in Atlanta, a city with a long and rich drag tradition, where his glamorous, big-haired, country-flavoured character Lurleen (all gingham check, frosted lipstick and saucy flirtations) hosted parties and lip-synced country ballads and quirky pop tracks. He was friendly with a scene of ambitious young American queens, who were then beginning to ride a new drag wave off the back of the club-kid phenomenon – queens like Lady Bunny, and another young queen who was then just about to cross over into the mainstream: RuPaul.

When I went to Tokyo I had no intention at all of doing drag, and assumed my brief, less-than-illustrious career as a badly painted mess was behind me. However, when Hallowe'en came around Angelo and I cobbled together a couple of silly nuns' outfits, Helen dressed up as a priest, and the three of us spent a drunken night in a men-only bar. It was a fun night and it would perhaps have finished there, except that a club promoter we knew bumped into us and suggested we do a show at his next party – and, as we have already learned, I'm easily led.

With some difficulty in petite-sized Japan, we managed to pull some kind of look together (mine decidedly less polished than Lurleen's), rehearsed a simple routine to an Abba number and turned up at the club with the track on a C60 cassette tape. Thinking I'd make a fresh start from the car crash art-drag I'd done in Dublin, I decided I needed a new drag name and, after spending no time at all thinking about it, chose 'Latitia' after a pet sheep we'd had when we were kids. So, Lurleen and Latitia did their first gig. Thanks, no doubt, to generous amounts of alcohol and ecstasy, people seemed to enjoy it and we were asked back. Before long we were doing small shows regularly in a few different clubs and having a blast. Helen made us matching outfits out of Hello Kitty fabric and we cobbled together backing tracks on a clunky old boom box. We practised dance routines in our little apartment, customised cheap accessories, learned the words to *The Brady Bunch* songs and spent the little we earned on taxis and getting high.

However, it soon became apparent that the names Lurleen and Latitia weren't working for us. Japanese people have great difficulty with the English letters *l* and *r*, finding them hard to pronounce or even differentiate between, so no one could remember our bloody names! We quickly decided we needed to come up with a 'group' name. Our *shtick*, our USP, was that we were foreign drag queens, so we decided we should pick a name that was English but at the same time easy for Japanese people to understand and remember.

We also wanted something that sounded 'cutesy' to appeal to the *manga* aesthetic so popular in Japanese youth culture and among the club-kids. The name we came up with was CandiPanti. It seemed to fit all the requirements, plus 'candy' and 'panty' were words that the Japanese already used, having adopted them from

English. Our intention was that CandiPanti would be our group name but that we would still be individually called Lurleen and Latitia. However, almost immediately people started to call Lurleen 'Candi' and me 'Panti'. It became a nickname that stuck until eventually even I forgot I'd ever been called anything else.

As for the surname 'Bliss'? One night after a gig, the club wanted me to fill out a payment form, which had a space for a family name. Until that moment, like Cher, I had never given a single thought to a surname so I put down the first thing that came into my head: Bliss. And for a short time thereafter I was 'Latitia Bliss', before poor old Latitia got entirely lost along the way and was usurped by a youthful Panti. (Clearly Latitia had never seen *All About Eve*.)

Panti isn't a name I would have chosen deliberately – when people hear it for the first time, they think I chose 'knickers' as a stage name and imagine all sorts about me and my show. And sometimes in 'polite company', especially on TV or radio, I hear a momentary awkwardness around my name, as if it might be salacious. When I first came back from Japan and it seemed like it might be a problem I started to use 'Pandora "Panti" Bliss', to give the false impression that Panti was short for Pandora, which worked to a large extent. I am still often referred to in that way and I don't disabuse anyone of the notion. I almost believe it myself at this stage. But, of course, it's almost impossible to shake a nickname and, anyway, in truth it's not a nickname any more and hasn't been for a long time. It's my name. I've embraced it. And, on the bright side, people don't forget it!

In those prehistoric early nineties, before YouTube and *RuPaul's Drag Race*, the only way to learn basic drag skills was through trial and error and, hopefully, from more experienced queens who were willing to give you the benefit of that experience. In the drag world it's an informal system known as 'drag mothers' where older queens pass on the tricks and secrets of the trade to favoured younger *gurls*. It's a kind of apprenticeship, and a young queen without a drag mother to teach her and help her up the drag-scene ladder in platform heels is unlikely to get far. Nowadays, many of the transformative secrets of the drag queen, from make up to hip padding, can be gleaned from the thousands of instructional YouTube videos on the subject but even today nothing beats a word of advice from a drag mother or simply being able to watch her get ready.

In Dublin I had fumbled through entirely on my own. I had never even *seen* an actual drag show. As a kid I had occasionally watched Danny La Rue on *The Royal Variety Performance*, and I was aware of Mr Pussy, whom I'd once seen interviewed on the telly, but I'd never met a professional drag queen or been to a show. Unlike neighbouring Britain, with its working-men's clubs and 'end-of-the-pier' entertainment, Ireland didn't have a popular drag tradition. My interest in drag as an entertainment form was simply because it seemed to me to be the logical result of the combination of the kinds of things that interested me: dressing up, making things, performing, camp movies, extravagant costumes. I just wanted to be one of the glove-wearing, cinch-waisted glamorous women who flounced petulantly across my Sunday-afternoon TV or poured from my subconscious onto my schoolbooks because, although they often looked bored, they never looked boring.

So, doing drag with Lurleen was a fun new revelation to me. I never considered her to be a drag *mother* – after all, she was only a couple of years older than me and thought of drag as a fun sideline rather than a career – but I did think of her as a drag 'older sister' and I learned a lot of the basics from her, like what kind of foundation or stockings to wear, or how to stack multiple pairs of false eyelashes. She also strongly influenced my early drag aesthetic of frosted eye shadow, big country-girl hair and short skirts, and through her I was exposed to a high-gloss, nightclub-based American drag style, which was very different from the English 'cock in a frock', or the panto dame we were more familiar with at home.

But the biggest thing I learned from doing drag with Lurleen was how much *fun* it was! At home drag had essentially been a solitary activity (and not necessarily even much fun). I wasn't part of any drag scene (there wasn't one to speak of) and I didn't have drag-queen friends to run around with, get drunk with and do silly shows with. I had enjoyed it as a creative project, in the same way that I had enjoyed art projects in college, but it wasn't *fun*. It wasn't running, screaming, laughing, sweating, falling over, boy-kissing, waking-up-with-bruises, attention-grabbing, outrageous *fun* the way it was with Lurleen. We were partners in mischievous cross-dressed crime, and we were game for anything.

We did silly, fun lip-sync shows in basement gay clubs and hostessed and acted the fool at mixed dance clubs. We performed at parties in art galleries and wound up in pop videos and magazine spreads. We paraded damply in the sweltering humid heat of Tokyo's first Pride parade and clambered giggling into cars with gangsters and tranny-chasers. We took ecstasy and smoked speed and fucked till we were sore, while club owners paid us to be the most fun, most outrageous people in the building and we were happy to oblige.

We had a regular gig at a cavernous club called Gold, spread over five massive floors in an awkward-to-get-to industrial part of the city, where achingly cool club-kids took ecstasy with fashion photographers and gangsters. There was a beauty parlour on one floor where two 'Harajuku Girls', with giant eyelashes, doll makeup and enormous platform boots, would smoke cigarettes and pretend to do hair and makeup while their friends sat around like extras from *Barbarella*. You could take an elevator up to the top floor, and when the doors opened, you found yourself standing in the front yard of a typical Tokyo suburban family home complete with kids' bicycles abandoned on the path. Inside you could hang out in the perfect-down-to-the-smallest-detail living room and play cards with 'Granddad' while 'Mama-san' got you a beer from the kitchen, or play computer games with the 'son' in his bedroom or giggle with the 'daughter' over the cutest pop star while flicking through magazines on her bed. This was 'bubble-economy' boom-time Tokyo, and if you wanted a suburban home complete with perfect family on the top floor of your nightclub you could have it.

In 1994 Cyndi Lauper – who was absolutely *huge* in Japan – came to Tokyo to promote a new album, and a single, which was a reggae-flavoured version of her classic hit 'Girls Just Want To Have Fun'. The video featured a gaggle of drag queens, and when she was booked to appear on a famous New Year's Eve TV show, which was to be pre-recorded, the TV company came looking for drag queens to provide colour for Cyndi's performance.

There wasn't much choice when it came to foreign drag queens in Tokyo, so Lurleen and I, along with a gang of Japanese queens and a couple of other foreign gays from the clubs (who were shoved into dresses and wigs and too-small shoes), ended up on TV dancing with Cyndi Lauper, pretending it was New Year's Eve, while a live studio audience of screaming Japanese girls flipped out. Cyndi was fun and sweet, but she was also all business – she was the boss: she knew what she wanted and expected to get it. And, luckily for us, I guess what she wanted was a couple of crazy messes full of vodka and LSD, because afterwards we were asked to do pretty much the same thing at her live gigs.

On the opening night in Tokyo Cyndi tripped onstage and awkwardly twisted her ankle. By the time she came off, it was swollen and painful, so the next night international superstar Cyndi Lauper was pushed around the stage in a feather-boa-covered wheelchair by two drunk drag queens in cut-off denim shorts. Coincidentally, Diana Ross was in town to do some gigs at the same time. After the show that evening the dressing-room door swung open and Miss Ross herself swept in. In a roomful of Japanese gays, she dramatically declared, 'RICE!' It turned out she meant Rest, Ice, Compression, Elevation, the recommended treatment for a sprain – a piece of advice I was unlikely to forget, given the circumstances. Indeed, over the years a number of clumsy limp-ankled gays at various parties have Diana Ross to thank for a speedy recovery.

Oddly, it was during my time in Japan that my friendship with my college pal Niall – the 'other gay' – was forged. I was having this chaotic adventure, one framed by nightclubs and drag, drugs and sex, and there weren't many people I knew who would appreciate the story I had to tell, cheer me on and not worry or lecture me. But Niall revelled in my adventures. So, this being the early nineties when the fax machine was the height of cutting-edge technology, I bought myself one and began sending him long handwritten, illustrated faxes that poured out of his office machine in Dublin at all hours, telephonically printed missives of ludicrous adventure from the other side of the world.

Tokyo, Japan, 1993

The club is big, and crowded. Metal tubing, pipes, machinery push through the concrete walls and thrust down from the floor above. On the dance floor the flashing lights pick out billows of dry ice and abandoned dancers. Pumping their bodies to the constant beat. The dark, the lights, the sweat, the beats, the smells … sensory overload. I'm leaning against the wall at the side of the dance floor. My heart is pounding with the music and I'm covered in dance sweat. A friend is beside me but we don't talk. Someone brushes by me and excuses themselves, 'Sumimasen.' It's a boy? A girl? Clad from neck to high-heels in black PVC, there are holes where the sweat and flesh are exposed. The face is painted and glittered. S/he continues on and disappears into the dark, the lights, the noise, the beat, the sweat, the dry ice.

A boy appears in front of me. He's nineteen, he's boyish, he's very pretty. I've slept with him before and he thinks he's in love with me. I haven't seen him in a few weeks and I haven't returned his calls. It doesn't matter. He puts his hands in my front pockets and kisses my neck. I smile at him but I don't move another muscle. He smiles back. Has he taken something or is it just the atmosphere, the sensory-disturbing lights? I can't tell ... the lights, my pounding heart, the dry ice. He leans himself along me and I can feel his erection. He kisses me on the mouth. He kisses my neck again. I let him, but I still don't move a muscle. I just smile. I don't move because I don't want to encourage him. I don't want him hanging off me all night. What if I see someone I really want? But I let him kiss me because he's pretty and sweet and has a beautiful small bottom. He mouths, 'What are you thinking about?' and I almost tell him. He moves to my side and links his arm through mine. I feel uncomfortable now. There is no sex in linking arms, only domestic bliss. I tell him I'm going to get a drink in a way that I know he won't follow me. I nod to my friend. A knowing grin and I move off into the bodies on the floor.

I pass a cute guy I know. He's holding a small laser in one hand. He smiles, a big cute smile, but doesn't wave. His left hand has no fingers and he keeps it in his pocket self-consciously. I smile back at him and consider kissing him ...

Maybe later. I need a drink.

The bar is populated with more of the same: the beautiful, the cool, the bizarre and the ordinary. I look at the drinks menu, and for the first time I notice they have Guinness. It's bound to be the awful Irish-coffee-tasting stuff I got once before in a bar in Tokyo, but the novelty of it amuses me so I ask for one. I get a blank look. They don't have it. I buy a beer.

I manoeuvre carefully back towards the dance floor, drink my beer down in two, then move onto the dance floor and begin to dance. At first with little effort or energy, but before long my body is jerking and pumping. The beat is loud and I can feel it inside me. I push my hand through my sweat-drenched hair, and though I can't see it, I know it sprays droplets over the people around me. How long have I been dancing? I don't know. I move across the floor towards where a wide, curving metal staircase winds up off the dance floor.

Upstairs where there is a cooler, quieter bar, I meet a girl friend and we sit and drink and talk. A transsexual woman leans over as she squeezes by and the nipples of her exposed breasts brush against my elbow. I talk to my friend about Ireland and Catholicism and abortion. The case of a fourteen-year-old Irish girl, molested and pregnant, is getting a lot of coverage in the international press here. The articles say things like 'in this ultra-conservative society' or 'it may be difficult for outsiders to grasp how much power the Catholic Church wields in this secular state'. The transsexual squeezes by again, though this time she is careful not to brush me with her nipples. She grins.

We make our way back downstairs. At the bottom of the stairs I feel the pressure of someone against my side. I look around. He's fairly attractive. I'd sleep with him. He's wearing a thick padded jacket in this heat. Outside it's snowing lightly, damply. I move my elbow and it presses against his flat stomach. A friend of his appears and talks to him. His friend looks just like him. I move my elbow away. He's acting cool towards his friend and glancing in my direction. His friend doesn't get the hint. I decide I'm too tired to play these Japanese-boy games anyway. I move away without looking back and into the thrusting, the sweating, the flick of girls' long black hair. Hands appear under my arms and press for my nipples. I take the hands in mine and turn around, knowing before I see him that it's the nineteen-year-old. He puts his hands on my neck and lets them slide down over my chest, my stomach, my crotch, my thighs. I smile. I kiss him on his soft lips, feel the smoothness of his chin, smile and turn and walk away. He pulls at my hand so I stop and start to dance. He dances energetically. He pauses to touch me from time to time. How long have we been dancing? I don't know. I turn and walk away. His head, his lovely pretty head, is tilted back. His eyes are closed, his head is all music. He doesn't notice me leave.

There is a guy blocking my way. I go to squeeze by him. He turns around: mid-twenties, the same height as me. Unusual for a Japanese. He's handsome. He smiles. I lean forward (I don't have to lean far) and I kiss him. His tongue is in my mouth. At first it's cool against my own warm tongue. He's been drinking something with ice in it. Something tangy. I can taste citrus and alcohol. Then it's warm. I feel his teeth with my tongue. I can feel the heat of his chest against mine. I can smell the sweat on his neck. I can feel the hardness of his erection against my hip, his hand in the small of my back, the edge of his eyebrow on mine, the sweaty moistness of his nose against mine. We separate and I smile. He smiles back and his teeth are caught in a flash of UV. It's a wolfish, sexy effect. I linger. His fingers touch mine. I move on.

A girl is looking at me as I begin to dance. I ignore her and dance, but she still manages to catch my eye again. She is moving to the music, but not a single bead of sweat mars her pretty face. Her hair (thick, long, glossy, black, like everyone else's) is pulled tightly off her face. She wears a black bra-top under a see-through shirt, and colourful, embroidered, heavily buckled pants, metallic earrings and a matching wrist cuff. Her eyeliner is thick, in perfect sweeps along her upper lids. She is looking appreciatively at my dancing. I give her the smile I use for just these occasions. The smile that says, 'You're very pretty, and I'm flattered, but I'm gay. Really gay.' She seems to understand. She smiles, she laughs, and jokingly imitates my dancing. I speak a few words to her. She's funny. What are we talking about? I don't know, remember. But she's funny.

I'm tired now. I move to the side of the floor and sit on a stool. My head back against the wall, my eyes closed. I can see, feel, smell (?) the lights flashing against my eyelids. I can feel the beat resonate in my chest. I can smell the heat, the smoke, the dry ice. I'm tired, my senses feel dulled but I feel very much alive. I don't seem to know which of my senses are sensing what. Am I smelling the sweat, or tasting it? Feeling it? Hearing it? I light a cigarette and take a deep drag. I feel it in my mouth, hear it in my throat, taste it in my lungs, I see it. I can feel the beat through the floor, through my dully-aching feet. I'm tired.

It's 5 a.m. on Friday morning. I'm tired. It's Tokyo. I'm tired. Time to go home. Where's that boy? The one with the citrus-coated tongue.

I had arrived in Tokyo full of the unbridled dangerous energy of youth – the kind of boiling, marauding energy that (as any horror fan will tell you) once unleashed can't be put back in its box and will either make you or destroy you. I was hungry for life, for experiences, for the *extra*ordinary. Not just hungry – ravenous. I wanted the whole world and I was going to have it even if it killed me. Painted and teased and tottering in heels, I tripped and ran and stumbled and crawled my way through emporia of night-time iniquity. I devoured everything I came into contact with, like a glamorous Ebola virus: art, drugs, boys, music, gangsters, dykes, drags, gays, love, sex, beauty. And my appetite was insatiable. No experience would be left unturned and no offer rejected. I lived my life by the adage 'Nothing ventured, nothing gained', and whatever murky situation presented itself, I simply asked myself, 'Have I done this before?' If the answer was, 'No,' then I threw myself into it head first and simply trusted I'd come out the other end. My constant mantra – and excuse – was 'Well, it'll make a good story.' It's not necessarily a course I'd recommend to everyone – there are times when I'm amazed I got out alive. Yet it worked for me, because when I finally stopped and looked in the mirror, I was a bit battered and bruised but, for maybe the first time in my life, the person looking back at me was me. Even under all the makeup.

Eventually, after four years, I ran out of steam. Or at least, life conspired to run the steam out of me. Helen had fallen in love with a handsome man from San

Francisco, whom she'd met at a club where CandiPanti were performing, and now she was planning to go with him to California. Angelo, who had always intended to pursue a 'proper' career in education, was considering returning to New York to take up a job opportunity at a university. And I had begun vaguely to consider the possibility that I might leave. I was comfortable there, though, had lots of other friends and I was still having lots of fun so I was in no immediate rush. Until I got sick.

At first I thought I just had the flu, but I couldn't shake it, and I became more and more tired, listless and achy. By then Angelo, Helen, our friend Hiroko, a French ex-boyfriend of mine and I were all living in separate small apartments in the same small 'traditional' block in the thick of things in central Tokyo. It was the perfect social living arrangement for a gang of twenty-somethings, with lots of running across the hall in a towel to borrow shampoo or stumbling in late at night and banging on Helen's door to tell her everything that had happened at the club in minute detail. All the apartments were similar: two rooms separated by a sliding screen, _tatami_-mat floors, a stow-away futon to sleep on, and a bathroom with a traditional Japanese hot tub. The apartment building was owned and run by Asakawa-san, a jovial, organised, nattily dressed older lady and her kindly retired-doctor husband, Dr Asakawa.

Asakawa-san loved to travel (she even eventually came to Ireland) and enjoyed having all these young foreigners in her building, taking a motherly interest in our lives and wellbeing. She worried about us and often asked after our own mothers. When I first began to feel seriously unwell, Asakawa-san was concerned, and it was Dr Asakawa who eventually told me I had hepatitis and would need to rest for a few months if I was to get better.

I was in my twenties and having the time of my life. I had hardly even heard of hepatitis, let alone knew that it was something I needed to be worried about, so it came as quite a shock to fun, stupid twenty-six-year-old me. There was no way I could lie in bed feeling miserable and not working for a few months in Tokyo. My paltry savings would be gone in no time and then what? I couldn't expect my friends to look after me for that long either. So, like any good Irish boy when he needs looking after, there was only one thing for it – home to Mammy. I was very ill and remember little of leaving Tokyo or getting home, but somehow between them, Angelo, Helen and Hiroko (and my older brother Lorcan who was regularly in Tokyo on business at the time) got me organised and home to Mayo, while a box with my meagre possessions was shipped on later.

9. My Mother's Exotic Bird

I SPENT MOST OF FEBRUARY and March of 1995 at home in Mayo, sleeping in my childhood bedroom, watching my parents' TV, eating my mother's brown bread and waiting for the lethargy of illness to lift, which it slowly did. During this period I was an outpatient under the care of a consultant at the hospital in Galway, and every few weeks my mother would drive me the thirty or so miles to Galway for my clinic appointment. It was on one of those drives that I sort-of-accidentally came out to my mother and nearly killed us both.

I know! You're thinking, *What?* How can his parents not have known he was a huge flaming queen? He practically had rainbow flags coming out his arse! And it's true, I practically did. Glitter-encrusted rainbow flags stapled to Liza Minnelli and Madonna.

It was all my older gay brother's fault that I hadn't come out yet. Lorcan isn't just seven gay years older than gay me, he's also the eldest child, the first-born, the

Golden Child, the gayer apparent. So, clearly, it was his gay responsibility – being seven whole years gayer than me! – to tell our parents that he, and we, were enormous homosexuals. This plan was clearly the natural order of things and, as such, was agreed to by the two of us. And it had been agreed to by the two of us *years before*! I had come out to my oldest sister, Auveen, when I was in my second year of college and she – emotionally – had called Lorcan in London to tell him the gay news, to which he replied, 'Me too.' It was a lot of gay in one day for poor Auveen. Soon after that the rest of our siblings knew (except the youngest, Clare, who was really pissed off with me later when she found out she was the last to know) and it was agreed by everyone that Lorcan should be the one to break it to our parents.

However, Lorcan kept putting it on the long finger, which was easy for him to do because he had lived abroad since he was fifteen and was rarely home to field questions from inquisitive neighbours or clutching-at-heterosexual-straws parents. And in an elaborate act of procrastination, Lorcan had decided that he wouldn't simply *come out* to our parents – no, his would be the most perfect and most perfectly executed coming out in the history of coming outs. His coming out would be the gold standard of parental coming outs to which all other coming outs would be compared in future generations. To do this, he set about researching the best way to come out by talking to his gay friends about the various ways they'd done it, and talking to their parents about how they wished it had been done. And after a supposedly exhaustive discussion, during which whole years passed, he decided that the very best way to come out was by letter. And he was right.

A lot of people imagine that the best way is to tell your parents to their faces. Surely that's the decent, brave and honest way, right? To look them in the eye and be a lesbian about it. It's not. When you look across the Christmas turkey at your parents in their naïvely cheerful paper hats and say, 'Mam, Dad, I'm gay,' you haven't just ruined Christmas dinner for everyone *again*, there's also a good chance you've ruined your relationship with your parents for another six months, because after your dad has stopped choking on the cranberry sauce he has to respond. He has to respond right there, right then, while the roast potatoes are going cold and your little sister's mouth is hanging open. And, given the circumstances, without a chance to digest this news, without a moment to consider it, to remember how much he loves you or to readjust how he has always imagined your future, and with you sitting there waiting expectantly, having brought you and him to this huge moment without warning, the chances are that he will say something he never would have said had he had time to think about it.

He might say something out of shock or embarrassment or anger, or perhaps something well intentioned but clumsy, and then you have to respond (from your indignant gay high horse) to his awkward response, and then he has to respond again, and before you know it, you're both caught up in a spiralling twister of unleashed gay emotion till you flounce off leaving your mother sobbing into the Brussels sprouts and a family tension that can take years to iron out. It takes most gay people years to come to terms with who they are, so it's hardly fair to expect your poor parents to leap immediately aboard the gay bandwagon with a rainbow flag and the lyrics to George Michael's cruising anthem 'Outside'. You are sitting there waiting for your poor parents to be the perfect Hollywood parents and say the perfect thing, as scripted by Oprah, but instead your dad opens his mouth and out falls a lump of stuffing, with 'You're queer?'

A letter gives your parents time to take in the news, adjust to the new reality, and carefully consider their response before writing back or picking up the phone. It greatly reduces the chance of someone saying something in haste that they'll later regret. Of course, these days it'd be an electronically instant email, which demands a speedy response in a way that a letter doesn't, but it's still better than sitting there daring your parents to be impossibly perfect.

Once Lorcan had decided that a letter was the best way to do it, he then set about procrastinating even further by writing the perfect coming-out letter. It was going to be a work of art, a masterpiece, the *Ulysses* of coming-out letters, but without the masturbation or the weird punctuation. Shakespeare himself would look at this letter and weep at its beauty. And so Lorcan spent months – no, years! – writing this perfectly pitched letter that struck exactly the right tone. He wrote it (he claims) and rewrote it (he claims) and left it on his chunky mid-nineties laptop on an aeroplane (he claims).

Meanwhile I was now spending an extended period with my parents for the first time in many years, vaguely avoiding topics of conversation that might stray on to awkward areas and slowly becoming more frustrated and annoyed by it. I felt I was hiding something from them, in a way being deceitful, and, unbeknown to them, it was coming between us. I say 'vaguely' avoided certain topics of conversation because through all of this I just assumed that really my parents already knew and were just waiting for me or Lorcan to tell them. I certainly knew that the possibility of Lorcan being gay had been discussed in the family long before we knew for sure, and I assumed that the same conversations had been had about me. After all, my parents knew about my college drag shows, and surely it wasn't going to surprise anyone that the artistic boy, who hated football and liked Martina Navratilova and drawing dresses, was gay. Surely you didn't have to be Jessica Fletcher to put that one together.

So, one bright West of Ireland spring morning my mother was driving me to my hospital appointment in Galway. I was feeling a lot better by then and we were

talking as we travelled along the familiar road (Galway
had always been our local town, where we went to do a
'big shop', get the sewing machine fixed or broken bones
plastered). My mother, in the context of some long-
forgotten conversation, said, 'Well, it's not like you came
home and told us you were gay and have AIDS.' And
in that moment, as my unsuspecting mother drove us
along the long, straight Curragh Line across the flat bog,
I *thought* what she was really saying to me was, 'I know
you're gay, son, so let's just get that out of the way, and
while we're at it will you just reassure me that there's
nothing more to worry about than a bout of hepatitis?'

And I, with some relief, replied, 'Well, I don't have AIDS
but I *am* gay,' and my mother nearly drove off the road.

It turned out that, bizarrely, my mother had never
thought I might be gay. I had so many girlfriends!
Apparently Lorcan had drawn all the gay suspicion.
Lorcan was probably the gay one and sure there wouldn't
be two gays in the one family so I was off the gay hook –
until I climbed up onto that gay hook and came crashing
through her windscreen on it just outside Galway.

After my mother had managed not to kill us both
by keeping us on the road, we spoke about it for *a
minute*. I don't remember what was said except that it
was awkward and weird, and *absolutely everything* that
Lorcan's letter was *not* going to be. In fact, it was worse
than that because even in Lorcan's worst nightmares he
had never imagined that leaving the coming out to me

might almost kill our mother in a car accident. And then my mother said she didn't want to talk about it any more. Or, at least, not yet. She needed time to let it percolate.

For three whole days we awkwardly didn't talk about it while all the while it loomed over the house like the world's most pregnant pause. My mother acted as if absolutely nothing had happened. I avoided being in the same room as her, and my father pottered about entirely oblivious.

Of course I knew that my mother was a devout Catholic, a woman who took her faith seriously and thoughtfully. Her bedside table was always weighed down with reading matter, and among it there were books of prayers or papal musings or theological treatises. She read at mass, spring-cleaned the church and was a minister of the Eucharist. The parish priest called in for tea, we said the Angelus at six o'clock, and confessed, confirmed and communioned more than was strictly necessary, but my mother's devoutness had never been overbearing. Sure as a kid I'd had no choice but to sit miserably through Sunday mass and go to confession in a creepy dark box with a musty-smelling old man and pretend to be sorry about things I pretended I'd done wrong, but I also had to brush my teeth and take a bath every Saturday, and so did every kid I knew. And when I was in my teens and I started to slack off going to mass there were some tense discussions and testing of boundaries, but I never felt I was being Bible-bashed.

She wasn't Carrie's mum. I never felt my mother's faith was *blind* faith. Her faith was considered and thoughtful and well read, and I assumed that when her faith, or at least the teachings of the Church, came into conflict with a real-world situation, like discovering your son was gay, my intelligent, reasonable mother would intelligently and reasonably discount those arcane teachings. She would simply make up her own mind.

But, not for the first time, I had underestimated the power of religion, because it turned out that my mother was having real difficulty in reconciling her faith with her gay son. On the morning of the third day, while my father was out at work, my mother called her brother. Uncle Brendan was an Irish Catholic priest in heathen England, a very different breed of priest from an Irish Catholic priest in holy Catholic Ireland. Before the implosion of the Irish Catholic Church from a seemingly never-ending string of abuse scandals and corruption, Irish priests tended to act as if they owned the place – because they did. Their authority was unquestioned; arrogance and self-entitlement were woven into their DNA. However, Irish Catholic priests in England were different.

Uncle Brendan was priest to a small, poor, sometimes discriminated-against minority community in a country of heathen Protestants, who viewed him with suspicion and sometimes derision. He didn't stride about like he owned the place while hats were doffed and indulgences sought – he schlepped about in his little car, part social worker, part local businessman, keeping the parish afloat by running the Catholic club attached to his church as a pub, wedding venue, bingo hall, dance hall and working-men's club. Uncle Brendan was a priest, and a realist. While a priest in Ireland could, until the nineties anyway, bleat on and toe the party line about contraception, divorce or homosexuality without looking ridiculous or laughably backward, because the state and its laws were aligned with this arcane world view, in England a Catholic priest had no such luxury. In Protestant England a Catholic priest had to make accommodation for condoms, the pill, divorces and queers because they were realities.

I don't know exactly what Uncle Brendan said to my mother when she called him but, whatever it was, it worked. It reassured her in some way, I guess (that I wasn't going to Hell? That I wasn't broken? That Mary Magdalene and I would have been great mates?), and when she put down the phone she was ready to talk.

We sat on my parents' bed and, like so many mothers before her, she cried. She cried for the loss of the future she'd imagined for me, she cried for what she thought would be a difficult path, she cried because she worried I'd grow old and lonely, like the gay people in books and movies, she cried (I guess) for the unknown, and she cried (I suppose) because she felt she didn't really know this new gay me. She cried for the imagined son she felt she'd just lost. And she cried because she loved me. And I cried because I loved her back.

We spoke about Lorcan, and after she'd talked to him on the phone and stoically taken on the full gay picture, we sat longer on her bed. Then she looked at me and said, 'You and Lorcan always seemed like two exotic birds that just landed down on top of us.' I knew exactly what she meant.

Still sitting on the bed, we heard my father's car pull up outside. My mother stood up, straightened her skirt and said, 'I'll go out and tell your father.' I sat nervously in the living room while my mother sat in the passenger seat of my father's car and told him about his two exotic birds.

Some minutes later he walked in the door, looked at me and said, 'Don't you be worrying about what I think,' then sat down for his lunch as if just being told by his wife that two of his three sons were gay was the least interesting thing that had happened all day.

In fact, he was *so* casual about it that, for a long time, I didn't fully believe it. My father had always been a calm, laid-back kind of guy but it hardly seemed credible that a sixty-year-old Irish Catholic man born in the 1930s could have been so entirely unfazed to hear that a third of his six children were queer, even if he'd had his own suspicions. For a long time I assumed that my father, seeing that his wife was upset, had decided to *act* completely unbothered for her sake. His utterly calm acceptance of the situation was, I decided, fake, a chivalrous façade designed to make it easier on his wife. However, in the years since I have asked him about it a few times and he has always insisted that he wasn't faking it. He simply didn't think it was anything to get upset over.

Of course now, in retrospect, I feel guilty for ever doubting him or worrying how he might react, but it's impossible not to. He's my father.

From that day my pre-war Irish Catholic father has never once betrayed any discomfort over his gay sons. Whether he's meeting boyfriends or sitting through a drag show that's much too loud, he does it all with the same vaguely bemused expression he has when the TV weather lady is wearing something he considers 'silly'. (In general, my father doesn't like anyone who appears on the telly but the poor posture and inappropriate fashion choices of lady weather presenters is his specialist subject: 'Oh, there's Slouchy again with her arms!')

My mother, like most parents, took longer to be totally comfortable. It had taken me a couple of years to come to terms fully with who I was and be at ease in my own gay skin, and my mother needed the same time. She never said or did anything that made her discomfort explicit, but I was aware of it. It wasn't easy for her to be totally at peace with having two gay sons. It was a difficult and painful journey for her, and for that I largely blame religion.

Religious people (including my mother) will always say how much comfort their faith brings them. They remember how their faith comforted them in sadness, how their quiet conversations with God helped them through difficult times, and how the rituals of religion strengthened them in bereavement. But they never describe the times their faith caused them unnecessary hurt. They never remember that, even though their love for their gay sons was never in doubt for even a second, and accepting their gayness should have been entirely simple and uncomplicated, it wasn't. It was not having gay sons that caused my mother pain, but having religion – and I have never forgiven religion for that.

10. Boom-town Gay

AS THE LETHARGY OF ILLNESS started to lift, I needed to make some decisions. What was I going to do now? Japan definitely felt like a finished chapter, but Dublin – the only place in Ireland I could have imagined living – didn't particularly appeal. After all, it was only a few years before that I had happily left behind its crumbling plaster and weird Lost World quality, where long-haired types with paisley shirts and guitars were still considered cool. Dublin was a town where nobody wanted to be Leigh Bowery and everyone wanted to be Bono. (Until some years later when Bono wanted to be Leigh Bowery for a while, but shortly after that everybody else stopped wanting to be Bono – it's the natural Irish cycle of things.) I had a vague notion I might go to Paris, but first I thought I'd go to Dublin, see old friends and hang out with Niall and his boyfriend Frank for a while.

Niall and Frank lived in a small Victorian terraced

house by the canal, just off the South Circular Road. Inside, Frank had stripped it completely, removed walls and doors, poured concrete floors, then got rid of the staircase and landing. He replaced it with a single sheet of perforated steel bent into steps, entirely without railing or support of any kind, which looked beautiful as it traced the outline of a staircase through space, but it quivered and wobbled and hummed as you went up or down it, hands out to balance yourself. At night in the dark a trip to the first-floor toilet from the first-floor bedroom meant a hazardous trip across thin air on an invisible gangway. In Niall and Frank's house drunk people slept on the ground floor.

For the next year or so I slept on the ground floor of Niall and Frank's house.

Dublin was changing fast. It was the early years of the Celtic Tiger and the city had a confidence and vibrancy it had never had before. For the first time in generations young people weren't leaving in their droves because they didn't have to. Not only that but other young people were arriving. Homosexual acts between men had been decriminalised in 1993 so the gay scene was slowly emerging from the shadows and the gay community becoming more confident. The dance-music explosion hit Dublin and straight kids started taking ecstasy and hanging out with the gays, everybody high on chemically induced love. Changes to the alcohol licensing laws meant you could now go dancing and drink beer and spirits, and new 'designer' clubs opened to cater to this new breed of dance-music clubbers. (Minsky's was discovered by straight kids as dance music and ecstasy hit Dublin in the nineties and was now a mixed dance club called Shaft.) For the first time ever, Dublin seemed like it could be just as fun as anywhere else. Suddenly Dublin had possibilities.

At the time Frank was the artistic director for a fashion company and he gave me a 'day job' in its flagship store, Makullas, on Suffolk Street, where I sold jeans to the city's new breed of clubbers and fashion kids, but my heart wasn't in it. I wanted to find a way to make dressing up and having fun pay. I needed to start climbing the drag ladder but the problem was there wasn't a drag ladder to climb. Dublin had no drag scene to get involved in. The gay scene pre-decriminalisation had been too small to support a professional drag one. There was Mr Pussy, of course, Ireland's 'leading misleading lady' who had arrived in Ireland from London in the seventies and become a household name, touring the bars and clubs up and down the country. At that time in the mid-nineties he famously co-owned his own riotous Mr Pussy's Café Deluxe with Bono, which became a late-night hangout and celebrity favourite where Pussy played bingo with the customers and late-night whiskey was sold in teapots.

But Pussy came from an English drag tradition of working-men's clubs and saucy humour and had made a career out of playing to mainstream straight audiences – there was even a slight coyness around his sexuality so as not to spook the punters – a world I knew nothing about and wasn't interested in. I wanted to continue doing the kind of clubbing drag I had done in Tokyo, where the audience was gays and club-kids and I was mostly getting paid to be outrageous and fun.

Besides, Pussy was an industry of one. There were no other professional working queens. There were a few fun gays who occasionally put on a show at The George or other gay bars, but they were doing it for the laugh and a few quid in drinking money. I wanted to find a way to make dressing up pay my rent, not just my pocket money. However, without a drag-scene ladder to climb, it looked like I was going to have to build my own as I went.

First, I had to get *any* kind of drag job. I found out what seemed to be the fun, *happening* club nights, and I went to all of them in drag and made myself the most fun, memorable person in the room. It wasn't hard – most of Dublin had never even seen a drag queen at that time. The most fun party at the time was a Monday-night party called Strictly Handbag at the Kitchen nightclub in Temple Bar, which attracted a very fun, mixed gay/straight crowd, which, as Monday-night clubbers usually do, took its fun seriously. For a few weeks I went every Monday and made myself the life and soul of the party, climbing on the bar, being fun and causing a commotion, and then I proposed to the promoter, Martin, that I would keep coming every week if he paid me. And, knowing a fun mess when he saw one, he did.

One small gig a week wasn't going to pay my rent but it was a start, and it was a laugh. I would run around with a Polaroid camera and take pictures with people – which, in the days before digital cameras and phones in your pocket, people loved – or pin badges onto them. I would pretend to do horoscopes (something I knew *nothing* about), dress up for holidays, crawl drunkenly along the bar or sit in a sun-lounger, wearing a bathing suit, under the street light at the club door. Basically, I made a fool of myself professionally and I was good at it. Soon I was hostessing in other clubs, like Pod, then the hottest club in town.

Pod attracted a fashionable, mostly straight but very gay-friendly crowd. Ecstasy was the drug of choice and straight-bloke van drivers would be hugging their new best gay friend they'd just met on the dance floor. I was younger and cuter and got hit on all the time by straight guys and tranny-chasers. Though I would flirt back, I rarely entertained them. The tranny-chasers were not really interested in having sex with *me* – they were just interested in having sex with my hair and my makeup and my nylons. They didn't really care if it was me under there or Dame Edna Everage! Occasionally though, one would come along who was so gorgeous that it would have been a gay crime *not* to sleep with him.

One evening a group of guys from a sports club were in and there was one among them from whom I immediately sensed a flirtation. He was movie-star handsome, tall and muscular, and at one point, after complimenting me for the umpteenth time, he quietly slipped his phone number into my handbag, making sure his team-mates were none the wiser. I couldn't believe my luck because he was totally, swoonsomely gorgeous and really sweet with it. The next day I called him and he invited me over to his place for dinner. I felt like I was going to the prom with the captain of the football team! I plucked and preened, dug out my sluttiest dress and wore two wigs for extra volume while Niall and Frank egged me on, then drove me to his building. (It turned out that he lived in a well-known apartment building in upmarket suburbia where a foreign ambassador had once shot himself, which I felt added a whole other layer of glamour to the occasion.)

Inside his place he was a real gentleman and treated me like the real lady he was so thrilled I actually wasn't, complimenting my dress and serving me wine in large glasses (which made my hands look smaller). A bottle later we started making out and had sex. At one point I wished I hadn't worn the second wig because as I fellated him the clips started to come undone and the second wig was flapping off his taut boxer's belly, like seaweed in a storm. Of course, in common with so many of his kind, what he really wanted was for *me* to make a lady out of *him* but, when I've spent two hours getting ready, and I look like a lady and smell like a lady, I think it's only fair that I should be the lady! Anyway, you try keeping a straight face, kneeling behind a huge hunk of a man, your nylons around your ankles and him on all fours, crying, 'You're my lady! You're my lady!'

When it came time for me to leave, he was suddenly concerned about being seen leaving his building with a huge transvestite so he asked me if I would change before he drove me home. In my innocence I agreed, which I now know to be a mistake, because most tranny-chasers don't like to be confronted with the reality behind the special effects. When I emerged from his bathroom in a pair of his old jeans and a T-shirt, with a freshly scrubbed face, he was mortified. That was too gay for him.

Even before I had left Japan, Niall had started to use pictures and images of Panti in his work as a graphic designer, and now that Panti was living in his house and running around nightclubs with him, he started to use her more – and has continued to do so for more than twenty years. I'm going to say that Panti is Niall's *muse*, because that suggests Panti's active participation in the creative process, sparking Niall's creativity, and therefore allows me to take some of the credit for some of Niall's incredible work over the years. However, the truth is probably closer to Panti being a more passive participant, Niall's 'fully poseable life-size doll', a shorthand symbol in his work for transgression and fun, a recurring motif. In truth it had little to do with me. I was just lucky that, for whatever reason, he liked to dress me up and make pictures with me in them. What is absolutely true, though, is that the visual image of Panti over the years, the way people imagine her, is as much the result of Niall's work as my own. She has been a collaborative project visually.

One of the first things Niall used Panti in was the posters for the 1995 Smirnoff Young Designer Awards, 'The Exhilaration of Liberty'. He photographed me crawling around his concrete living-room floor in bra and knickers, then superimposed me crawling up Dublin's iconic Liberty Hall, a drag Godzilla, curly red hair tumbling down my back. I played some small role at the awards themselves, and it was through this that I first met a tall, fashion-obsessed Trinity student called Enda McGrattan, who was producing the event. Enda would become a great friend, but would also later become Veda Beaux Reves, an iconic drag figure on the Irish gay scene, and one of my drag-partners-in-crime for many years.

At Christmas Niall and Frank decided to use Panti as the Christmas decoration for the big store Frank ran. Niall designed ads featuring Panti dressed as Santa and soon 'Panti Claws' could be seen all over the city on the sides of buses. On the outside of the store's five-storey building, a giant twenty-foot-tall Panti loomed out over the street wearing white ice skates and a red fur-trimmed skating dress. The skirt was very short so pedestrians got an eyeful of Giant Panti's black knickers, and one day a very angry woman stormed into the store to complain because she thought the black knickers were Panti's bush!

Rory O'Neill

In one of the store's big windows Frank installed a huge metal swing in the shape of a bell, and on Thursdays, Fridays and Saturdays of the Christmas period I would sit in the swing, wearing my Panti Claws outfit and lip-sync Christmas songs. Frank also installed an intercom system and people outside on the street could talk to me, which mostly involved kids making farting noises. It all caused quite a commotion. The bus stop across the road was temporarily moved so passengers (and the drivers) could get a better view, and sometimes huge crowds would gather outside, spilling into the street and blocking traffic. Bizarrely, people were sometimes not sure if I was actually real. One evening I was swinging back and forth to Eartha Kitt's 'Santa Baby' when a woman's hand slowly sneaked its way through the curtain behind me, felt around till it found my ankle and squeezed. Then it disappeared in a flash and a broad Dublin accent from the other side of the curtain cackled, 'It *is* bleedin' real!'

Niall and I were friends with an earthy, bossy, gregarious straight girl called Claire Crosby, who had a mouth like a sailor and a mischievous attitude, and somewhere along the way the three of us decided we should start a club night together. For the fun. Our motivation was never about making money – there are easier ways to do that than in the notoriously fickle world of clubbing. We were interested in having fun, in making things, and in *not being boring*. Being boring was our great fear and boredom our great motivator. Not being boring had become a kind of mantra. Bill Clinton had his 'IT'S THE ECONOMY, STUPID'; our bumper sticker was 'DON'T BE BORING'.

Somewhere *else* along the way, no doubt fuelled by booze and one-upmanship, we decided it should be a fetish club. None of us had any particular interest in or knowledge of the fetish scene but that didn't stop us. In fact, in those pre-internet days we weren't really sure if there even *was* a fetish scene in Dublin, but that was exactly why it seemed like a good idea – it wasn't boring.

However, when we went to London and checked out a few big fetish events and spoke to people in Dublin's sex shops, one of the things that struck us was that, actually, the fetish scene seemed ... well ... a little boring. People took it all rather seriously. It came across as quite po-faced and it just didn't seem that much fun. If we were going to run a club night it needed, most of all, to be fun. It needed a sense of humour.

We called it GAG. The first job was to find a venue for it, which was relatively easy in those early days of the Celtic Tiger. There were still plenty of dingy, half-empty venues around town with owners willing to let us try to fill them with whatever craziness we were planning while they waited for some developer to come along and buy the place to build offices or a shopping centre. The problem was *keeping* the venue after they'd seen what we were actually up to.

We held the first event at the Tivoli on Francis Street and spent the day unscrewing light bulbs, covering everything in PVC, stretching rubber sheets from the ceiling and wrapping everything with construction tape. We put an ad for the party in the small ads in the back of *The Irish Times* (because we assumed it would be the paper of choice for the pervert set) but when Frank called to place the ad, the woman in the advertising sales department assumed that GAG was an acronym and wouldn't take the ad till Frank told her what GAG stood for. With no time to think Frank said, 'Eh ... It stands for Gays Against Germaine Greer.' She was happy with that and the ad went in. We covered the city in mysterious GAG stickers, handed out beautiful kinky-looking fliers and told everyone who would listen it would be a party like Dublin had never seen. And it almost was.

The people who turned up were all sorts: gay, straight, older, younger, fashion types, perverts, students and businessmen, and we welcomed them all, as long as they passed the 'fetish' dress code. We were pretty relaxed about how people interpreted it – partly because we were trying to grow an almost non-existent scene and didn't want to scare people off who didn't have 'traditional' fetish gear (leather, rubber, etc.) but also because we figured a nutty mix of people would be more fun. So, if you turned up to the club in a rubber nurse's outfit or a gas mask, in drag or riding boots and a tweed jacket, it was all fine with us, so long as we believed that *you* believed it was sexy. And if someone turned up wanting to come in in regular street clothes we told them they could if they stripped to their underwear. And most of them did.

At that first party Niall and I did the first of what would become infamous GAG performances and it set the template for the rest that would follow. We knew that we wanted to do something that would slightly shock people but at the same time make them laugh. Something they would gleefully recount to open-mouthed friends the next day. I don't remember who first suggested that Niall should pull a six-foot-long string of pearls from Panti's ass but, whoever it was, I, as usual, agreed to do it because ... well, because it wasn't boring. Anyway, it wasn't really such a crazy idea, as far as I was concerned. Leigh Bowery had given himself enemas during some performances, and during a student summer in London I had once seen legendary New York performer Lactating Lady Hennessy Brown in Heaven, where, before squirting the audience with milk from her legendary lactating breasts, a man put his head between her legs, emerged with a string between his teeth and backed all the way across the crowded dance floor with it until eventually she released it with a flourish. Then she did 'the crab' and blew out flaming torches with her pussy. No one could accuse Lady Hennessy of being boring.

Of course, there were logistics to work out first, so I bought a long string of cheap plastic display beads and set about experimenting, disappearing into the bathroom to work it out (or, perhaps I should say, 'work it in') before backing into the living room to show my handiwork to a cackling Niall and Frank. Then there was the problem of how to show the, eh, *mechanics* of the performance to all sides of the room so we got a heavy-duty electric rotator (the kind they use to slowly turn cars around in showrooms) for Panti to perch on.

And so I found myself in a cold, cramped club toilet awkwardly douching with cold water before lubricating a string of plastic pearlescent beads and slowly (and carefully!) inching them into my ass till there were only a couple of inches of pearly tail left hanging out. Then, dressed in a short black slip, stockings, suspenders and a black jockstrap, I took to the stage, perched daintily on all fours on the rotating stand, my rosy rump presented and slowly scanning the room with its pearly eye. While I dramatically lip-synced to Édith Piaf's 'Non, Je Ne Regrette Rien', Niall – dressed all in black rubber and calling himself 'Mr Sphincter' – slowly and teasingly (and, dare I say, *lovingly*?) pulled the beads from my ass, swung them over his head and tossed them into the gob-smacked crowd as Piaf crescendoed. Veda Beaux Reves claims the flying beads wrapped themselves around her then-innocent boy-neck but I think she just says that to be nice. I hope it's true because, if it is, it's sweet that we later became great friends and drag sisters after such auspicious beginnings.

We called the performance 'Pearl Harbor' and it did everything it was meant to do. The club was the talk of the town the next day, but more than that, the performance set the tone for the party. When people see a performance like that in a club it gives them permission to let their hair down. It gives them licence to be licentious. If everyone has just watched a drag queen have a string of pearls pulled out of her ass to the strains of France's national treasure they aren't going to be bothered if you get a little wild on the dance floor or hook up with some hot guy in a toilet cubicle. So people did. The only problem was that the management and staff of the Tivoli weren't used to finding a corseted woman giving some bloke a good trashing with a riding crop in a corner of the dance floor, or walking into the toilet to find all the bulbs had been removed and rubber-clad guys were having sex with each other in the dark. So, even though the party was a success, we had to find a new venue.

We went through three venues before we found one that was happy to have us. The club was owned by one of the ponytailed young businessmen who were beginning to emerge in the economic boom. Unfortunately for him, his club had developed a reputation after it had been adopted by one of the city's most notorious criminal gang families as a hangout, and there was nothing he could do about it. Nobody messed with that family and no bouncer in his right mind was going to refuse them and expect to be able to walk home from work. There wasn't much the gardaí could do about it either. The story goes, whether true or not, that eventually his security people turned to those who *could* do something – the IRA, who conveniently weren't too busy at the time because they were not long into their ceasefire. New bouncers started to work at the club, who had a few quiet words, and the criminal family set up shop somewhere else. By the time we arrived, looking for a venue, the club was rid of its criminal problem but was still struggling to overcome its reputation, and the management's attitude was 'If you can get people in here you can do what you want.'

The club was in the Docklands, on a part of the quays that is now all shiny glass office blocks and gleaming desirable apartment buildings, but at the time was a fairly bleak, dark part of town full of old warehouses, the odd dodgy character and the occasional slow-moving car. Back then, it seemed far out from the city centre, a damp trek along the quays at night. The location would have been a drawback to most other parties, but it worked in our favour – it added a certain *frisson* of danger, and it was away from prying eyes. No one was going to stumble across it accidentally so you didn't need to worry that your boss might happen upon you in your leather harness unless he wanted to.

Once a month a group of us would spend hours plastering the walls with graphic or silly sex words, hanging slings and meat hooks from the ceilings, filling old tin shower cubicles with foam, building makeshift darkrooms, mounting slide projectors, painting walls and generally destroying the place. And every month more and more fun-loving perverts would turn up. There were the professional perverts – straight women in shiny latex, gay men in leather harnesses, lesbians in sharp suits with fat cigars, straight men in studded collars, transvestites in thigh-high PVC boots – but there were also half-naked clabbers in homemade outfits, nervous office workers in football gear, adventurous farmers up from the country, and excited beer-couraged straight guys, who'd heard something wild was going on down the docks. And if that straight guy seemed easy-going and nice and was prepared to strip to his underpants, we let him in.

Inside, elderly transvestites would be chatting at the bar with a straight woman, who was nonchalantly tugging on her husband's leash, while shaven-headed gay boys in rubber and tattoos made out on the dance floor, and a straight businessman in a corset engaged in conversation with legendary Dublin DJ Tonie Walsh, who was holding forth while lying in a bath full of jelly.

In a sign of the times, I had first met Tonie at the funeral of a mutual friend who had died of AIDS. Tonie had turned up looking for all the world like an American Indian from the Saturday-afternoon movies of my youth, his long, straight hair dyed pitch black, his aquiline nose summer-tanned, and a dramatic scar (with an appropriately dramatic story) etched across his cheek. I didn't know it then but Tonie's indefatigable enthusiasm for life and hedonism, and his ability to turn up at every event in an outfit he had spent a week making out of chicken wire, plastic, papier-mâché and resin, would make him a permanent fixture in my life for the next twenty years.

Niall's and my performances, mostly based around pulling things from my ass, became much-talked-about focal points of the parties, and as time went on we had to get creative about what was coming out of my ass and how.

So, I have squatted over an inflatable globe while emoting to the dulcet tones of Karen Carpenter singing 'Top of the World' and squirted out milk, which sprayed off the North Pole and covered the front row of perverts in a fine milky mist. I've douched with poster paint (non-toxic!) and splashed out onto canvases that were then auctioned to the assembled clubbers. I've had minced meat shoved in one end, a handle turned on my back, and a string of sausages pulled out the other. I've even dressed as a secretary perched at her typewriter lip-syncing to Dolly Parton's '9 to 5' while a suited Mr Sphincter pulled the lyrics of the song from my shiny rump, like a perverse karaoke machine. Though just the chorus because, after all, it was my ass and not the Port Tunnel. We'd actually spent a lot of time trying to work out a way to get the lyrics up my ass, then back out again on cue in a readable form. Which is more difficult than you might at first imagine! Eventually we printed the lyrics on a long thin strip of paper that we then rolled up and put inside a soft rubber cup-type thing we'd found (which had a wide lip to prevent any sudden disappearances!). I then *very* gingerly (with paper cuts in mind!) popped the whole lot up my bum, leaving the mouth of the rubber cup accessible, with the end of the paper strip hanging out like an eager dog's tongue. In rehearsal it all worked perfectly, and when Dolly hit the chorus and Mr Sphincter pulled, the lyrics appeared perfectly on cue. But when we did the actual performance, I think I must have rolled up the lyrics a little too tightly because when Mr Sphincter pulled, the lyrics appeared from my end like a long, pointy, uncoiling paper cone, extending from my glossy rump like an alien horn until eventually it reached the point of no return and collapsed in a tangled mess on the stage. No one seemed to mind. I think the perverts were just happy to be out of the house.

To celebrate the club's birthday we turned the tables, and with a rubber-clad Mr Sphincter on all fours, I messily and stickily made a cake out of him, dumping big bowls of cream, custard, jelly, and hundreds and thousands all over him before finally shoving a candle up his ass and lighting it – somewhat awkwardly because my hands were covered with sticky trifle.

At one point we were invited to perform at a huge fetish event in London, and after doing 'Pearl Harbor' on a stage in the middle of a crowded warehouse, we finished with the cake performance. However, this time we upped the ante with an impressively large candle – the end of which we carved so Niall could accommodate it – and after I had somewhat roughly shoved it into a caught-off-guard Niall, I momentarily turned my back to get the lighter to light it. When I turned back, lighter in hand, Niall was there on all fours, covered with curdling cream, looking at me with big eyes ... There was no sign of the enormous candle. I looked around in a panic only to realise that, the moment I had turned my back, Niall had spasmed: it had shot out of his ass, flown over the front row and taken out a latex-clad hairdresser from Leeds.

I never asked the bouncers if the story about the IRA was true but, whether it was or wasn't, they took everything in their stride, watching it all with an air of bemused amusement. It was an easy gig for them, of course. The fetish crowd tend to be a very relaxed, polite, live-and-let-live bunch, the club-kids and the gays were just out for a fun time, and the transvestites were just thrilled finally not to be the weird ones in the room. There was never any trouble. The head bouncer, a big shaven-headed older bloke, had an avuncular air about him and late one night after we'd closed I found him – office stapler and black plastic bin bags in hand – stapling together a basic outfit onto a fully naked older drunk guy, who had somehow managed to lose all his clothes. Then, pointing him in the direction of the city centre, he stood and watched, like a concerned parent sending their kid off to school on their own for the first time, as Naked Guy wobbled and rustled his way along the quays in his shiny new bin-bag couture.

Dublin had never seen anything like it, and we were the talk of the town. Half the stories people heard weren't true, of course, but we weren't going to disabuse anyone of their fevered notions. In a bar one evening a guy told us that he'd heard 'on very good authority' that Claire Crosby had had to get the ceilings in her house reinforced because of all the sex contraptions she was hanging from them. She loved that.

All the talk and fevered gossip was good for business but eventually it started to bring us unwanted attention. The tabloids started to write salacious *faux*-shocked stories, culminating with the British *Sunday People* splashing a breathless front-page story, 'DUBLIN SEX ORGY SENSATION!', complete with 'RED HOT PICTURES INSIDE!'. The press attention brought closer scrutiny from the gardaí, who didn't seem to know exactly what they should do about us, if anything. Eventually, though, notoriety started to make things more difficult, so when the building looked like it was going to be sold, as the Celtic Tiger got its teeth into the Docklands, it seemed a good time to move on and do something new.

We approached John Reynolds, the owner of Pod (where I had been hostessing and performing), about doing an old-school, sweaty-dance-floor gay night on Fridays. He was open to it, but first he had another suggestion. Building work was nearing completion on a big new venue in the old railway station above Pod, and though it had been designed as a live venue with a huge, high main room, a big stage, and a large balcony, John was interested to see if and how it might be used as a club space. He would give us Friday nights in Pod's old railway tunnels if, first, we did something large-scale in the new venue – and that sounded fun to us.

A big space like that was going to need a lot of people to fill it, so we had to do something with broader appeal than a straight-up fetish party. Basically we decided on a more colourful, lighter version of GAG. We would keep some of the elements that made it fun – the dressing-up, the performances, the mixed crowd, the sexiness and the silliness, and throw glitter on them. We would put GAG in drag, and call it Powderbubble.

Powderbubble would be a much bigger project but there was no shortage of young and creative people wanting to get involved. Soon it wasn't just Niall and me but a growing family of people who liked to make stuff and do things. It was still early in the boom years, before everybody had full-time jobs and go-getting careers and couldn't stop, gotta go, chat soon, because there was money to make and even more to borrow. There were still plenty of poor students and underemployed young people, with the time, energy and inclination to get involved in stuff just for the fun.

Dublin in the mid to late nineties was a city falling in love with itself. The boom was beginning to steam out of the station, picking up speed as it went and pulling everyone behind it in its draught. There was a sense of possibility about the place and a confidence we'd never had before. The city was changing before our very eyes –

shiny new buildings were going up everywhere, bridges were being built, rail links were being planned – and we were changing with it. The mad rush to get off the island had stopped because, for the first time ever, we actually believed it was as good as anywhere else. We stopped looking across the water at London or Barcelona or New York, and stopped apologising for being from Dublin. Sure wasn't the whole world Riverdancing.

Of course, in time the country would lose the run of itself and we'd get our comeuppance for daring to believe things were going to work out, but for a few innocent years it really did feel like it was all going to end happily ever after.

From the beginning Powderbubble was a success, and roughly every month through 1997–8 Niall would design a beautiful, expensive, unusually shaped flier, and come up with a (slightly) tongue-in-cheek grand vision for the next event: 'ELASTICK FUTURE PLASTICK FANTASTICK, THE FUTURE TESTAMENT, FUTURE FROSTED FLESH FANTASY, FUTURE HARVEST ...' We were very big on 'the future'. Apart from 'not being boring', our other constant refrain was 'Never look back, only forward!' And I mean that literally. We actually used to say it all the time.

Someone would have an idea for a performance or club decor and someone else would shoot it down, saying, 'No! Never look back!' It was our obsession with looking to the future that made us violently anti-draping.

We were always covering things – stages, scaffolding, balconies, doors – but we refused to drape anything. We lived in horror of draping! When we covered things (usually with shiny coloured PVC) we stretched it tight, neatly stapled down the corners and obsessed over hard edges. Soft draping was for the fusty, stuck-in-the-mud, sexually repressed Victorians: *we* were thrusting into a shiny, glowing, straight-lined pansexual future. Or something like that, anyway.

There was a group of maybe ten of us, but on the day of a Powderbubble lots of volunteers would turn up – students, gays, club-kids – happy to help out in return for nothing more than guest list and maybe a few beers. All day we'd build scaffolding, wrap (not drape!) furniture, build installations, hang projectors, mount screens, and struggle with huge inflatables. We knew every hardware store in town intimately: we were never without a cable-tie, we had a favourite brand of gaffer tape, and someone was always shouting over the noise of the power drill, 'Who took the good stapler?' Driven by Niall's perfectionism, we obsessed over everything being *exactly* right. We developed communal OCD. A couple of people would spend the whole day on their backs on top of a scaffold slowly hanging a perfect grid of leaping inflatable dolphins (spray-painted silver, of course) on cat-gut from the ceiling over the whole venue, and if even one of the shiny cetaceans was as much as a couple of inches too high or too low, everyone would look quietly disappointed and wonder who was going to mention it. Eventually they moved the scaffolding, climbed back up, and adjusted the rogue plastic bottlenose.

No idea was too big to consider. For one party we decided to turn the whole venue into a forest so we tracked down a tree surgeon and a truck and got a few trees, which we then installed in the venue. It was beautiful, more magical than we'd even imagined – until the fire officer turned up an hour before we opened and practically had a stroke.

'You've basically filled the whole place with firewood! Someone could die.'

'Well, at least they'd die somewhere pretty!'

We were made to take the whole thing down, which we thought was an outrage. These jobsworths just didn't understand art!

And, of course, there were performances and 'happenings'. There were drag queens riding giant inflatables or rolling across the floor in huge clear plastic balls. There were people in papier-mâché heads making cakes, and mermaids manning nail bars. I sang with a rock band made up of teenagers in their school uniforms, and threw a bloody pig's heart at Shirley Temple Bar while we both danced on crutches and sang 'Don't Go Breaking My Heart'.

For one of the parties we decided to do a homage to the famous photograph of Bianca Jagger riding a white horse into Studio 54. First we had to find a horse but a few phone calls later that turned out to be easier than we'd imagined. On the day, a cheery woman turned up with the white horse and assured us that the animal would be fine to walk into the club through the side doors and onto the dance floor with Panti on its back. We did a rehearsal, with the woman leading the horse, and I doing my best Lady Godiva, wearing little more than a few ivy vines and a lot of hair, and the horse acted as if it wandered through nightclubs all the time.

I worried that the horse might not be so relaxed later when the club was full of people and noise, but the owner assured me that this horse was virtually unspookable. And she was right. Later that night the horse seemed almost bored as it carried me through the loading doors from the car park, around the bar, across the dance floor of startled clubbers and to the front of the stage, where I dismounted and launched into a number.

In fact, it all went so smoothly and calmly that the following Christmas we decided to do it again, this time with Panti dressed as the Virgin Mary on a donkey. Some phone calls were made, a donkey was procured, the rehearsal went smoothly, and our confidence was high – until showtime. The club's side doors were opened with a dramatic flourish and fifteen hundred expectant clubbers turned to see what was going on, only to discover Panti atop a donkey that had decided to act in accordance with its species' reputation. It dug in its hoofs and refused to budge a single inch as its handler pulled it and coaxed it, and I tried to jiggle it forward while clasping a swaddled Baby Jesus to my bosom. After a minute or two, when it was clear that the donkey was not to be persuaded, and the fifteen hundred clubbers were now more bemused than expectant, I slid off its back and, with whatever drunken dignity I could muster, walked into the club.

While Powderbubble continued roughly once a month in the old railway station, Niall and I started our weekly gay night in the tunnels underneath it. H.A.M. was a music-driven, cruisy, sweaty, old-school gay night and it paid my rent for the next eight years. Of course we were, as ever, very concerned with how it looked, so every Friday Niall and I, with DJ Tonie Walsh and our friend Karim, would spend the day turning the tunnels into various visual gags – one week the place would be the inside of an aeroplane cabin and the next it would be a sexy/kitschy farm. Its first incarnation was as a butcher's abattoir and we hung huge pieces of 'meat' and heavy plastic freezer curtains everywhere while Niall, Karim and I walked around wearing nothing but white rubber butcher's aprons, white rubber boots and lots of fake blood. We went round the city tagging everything with big stickers that said 'BUTCHER QUEERS', which we thought was a clever word play but which horrified two American tourists. They started lambasting us, thinking we were organised queer-bashers. In another incarnation, we mischievously and defiantly turned the place into a pharmacy with huge foam capsules of AZT (the infamous HIV drug) hanging from the roof.

Eight years is an eternity in Clubland, and a whole generation of gay Dubliners grew up on the dance floor at H.A.M. People fell in and out of love there, they shagged and argued there, they danced and drank and took ecstasy there, they made new best friends and remembered old ones, they laughed and cried and fought and stormed off in a huff and kissed and made up. They lost wallets and dignities and virginities and minds there.

One night we were looking after the Spice Girls, who turned up at the height of their fame, and the next week we were trying to stop a very angry African guy beating up one of the street 'girls': it wasn't till she brought him into the club and into a toilet cubicle that he discovered to his (hard to believe) surprise that 'She has a pen! She has a pen!'

Over the next ten years or so I was involved in a long and varied list of clubs and parties as a promoter, hostess or performer, and usually as some combination of all three. Some were long-running, others short-lived; some were big club events, others small midweek get-togethers. Even though Niall moved to London, he continued to design the graphics for every one.

For a couple of years at H.A.M. we ran a cabaret called Gristle earlier in the night as a pre-club entertainment. I emceed and performed, and every week was joined by various queens from what was the first wave of drag performers, who were emerging and creating a new Dublin drag scene: people like Shirley Temple Bar, Veda Beaux Reves, Dizzy Dyin'forit, Dolly Grip, Katherine Lynch, Annie Balls, Siobhan Broadway and more. It was at Gristle that I first started to push my stage act into storytelling and stand-up. Up till then my act had been almost entirely visual, designed for noisy nightclubs with makeshift stages and easily distracted drunk patrons with short attention spans. My club act was drawn with broad brushstrokes, all dramatic lip-syncing, visual gags and wild energy, and although I loved it, it had begun to feel limiting. In a sense I was trapped by the pre-recorded soundtrack, unable to veer from the original plan or react to the unexpected in a *live* way. In a sense the audience members were passive viewers, watching my show like a cinema audience, and I was like an actor on a movie screen, following the script even if a fire broke out in the stalls.

So, at Gristle, where the audience were seated and not yet drunk, I talked to them. I told comic stories or ranted about whatever was annoying me. I put my four years at art college to some use and, with an easel on stage, I illustrated as I went. I read *Butler's Lives of the Saints* and regaled the audience with the life stories of the most outrageous and ridiculous saints. I retold Bible stories from a gay perspective and told silly 'stories' in a fake language parody of modern Irish. I wandered through the audience asking questions, slagging and cajoling, and at times it feels like I haven't shut up since.

It was around this time that Shirley, Veda and I formed our 'girl group', SugarRush. We did all sorts of gigs, from scary dives with sticky carpets in Derry, where we were expected to perform standing in the corner with no lights and a ceiling so low our wigs kept getting caught, to fancy ladies-who-lunch charity fundraisers, but it was the corporate gigs (especially the Christmas parties) that were our bread and butter. We'd turn up with the show on CD, a group number to start and finish, a couple of solos each in the middle, and after everyone had had their dessert and too much wine, we'd do our best to entertain bleary-eyed Helen from Accounts and Phil from Sales while struggling with crappy sound and awful lighting in a hotel function room.

Those gigs taught me to appreciate one of the intrinsic advantages of performing in drag: it gets people's attention. One Christmas I was booked for a big corporate party at the Great Southern Hotel in Galway. It was a huge affair with hundreds of people being served dinner on long tables that ran the length of the enormous room, and even more people eating on a balcony. There was other entertainment on the bill – fire-eaters outside, a close-up magician going round the tables and, this being Galway, a puppeteer, who was interacting with the hapless diners – but the heavy lifting was to be done by a young up-and-coming comedian, who would have been well known in comedy circles at the time but not to most of the alcohol-reddened-cheek owners in that room.

By the time he stepped onto the stage, he was facing a sea of askew paper hats, and the noise was deafening: roast-beef dinners were served or cleared, cutlery was clanked, while conversations and good-natured insults were shouted across tables. It was impossible. One half of the massive room were only vaguely aware that there even was a comedian. I watched through my fingers from the back of the upstairs balcony, as the noise level got higher and higher as even the guests who wanted to hear him gave up trying. He could have been the greatest stand-up the world had ever known and not a single person in that room would have known or cared. I felt bad for him – until I remembered I was next.

I was to go on during dessert, tell a few jokes, do the raffle. I knew I could get plenty of laughs out of picking out prizes and teasing winners, but not if nobody realised I was there, so when I walked into the room I was dreading it – but I had an advantage over the comedian. I had drag. I was six foot ten in platform heels and big hair, wearing a short yellow dress with bell sleeves and ice-cream cones printed all over it, and I was painted up like a stolen car. I was hard to miss or ignore (even from the far end of the room) and the hubbub of conversation died away as people started to crane their necks to get a look at the giant candy-coloured cartoon that had just walked in.

Turned out I'd done half the work by the time I'd left the dressing room.

11. All Dressed Up and Somewhere To Go

IN 1987 NIALL AND FRANK had helped to produce a small, wonderfully ridiculous event in Sides nightclub called the Alternative Miss Ireland. A fundraiser for the Rape Crisis Centre, it had been inspired by an annual party thrown by English artist Andrew Logan, which took the staid, old-fashioned format of Miss World and threw it to a pack of gay wolves. It became a wild, outrageous, eccentric costume competition: people of all genders and none would take to the catwalk in elaborate costumes for daywear, swimwear and eveningwear. After struggling into their costumes under the stairs, seven or eight contestants took to the small stage in Sides to be interviewed by Linda Martin. Then she and Mr Pussy, the judges, crowned Miss Isle, a naked guy covered in paint with a cardboard nuclear missile thrusting from his crotch (this was the era of Cold War politics and impending nuclear holocaust), as the first Alternative

Miss Ireland. Tonie Walsh, who had entered wearing a costume inspired by Rathmines Town Hall with a clock tower balanced on his head, was narrowly edged out.

Nine years later Niall, our then newly acquired friend and collaborator Trish (who'd just arrived in Dublin after a few years' squatting, photographing and clubbing in London) and I were approached by Dublin AIDS Alliance, a volunteer organisation that worked with people living with HIV / AIDS, and asked if we would produce a new Alternative Miss Ireland to raise funds for them. It sounded like fun to us so we agreed. Had we known then that it would end up consuming a huge amount of our time and energy for the next seventeen years we might have hesitated.

The 'pageant' would be open to all ('men, women, animals', we declared) and would be a modern, 'post-gender', tongue-in-cheek gay take on Irishness. It would be, we told everyone, a cross between Miss World, the Rose of Tralee, the Calor Kosangas Housewife of the Year, and that time in college we bunked off art history class and took mushrooms. There would be three rounds, and each contestant (each 'Miss') would perform twice – once in daywear and once in eveningwear. The swimwear round would be an interview. We were determined that there would be as few rules as possible and we would do our best to accommodate any contestant's ideas, no matter how insane. This event would be all about encouraging creativity and nuttiness and outrageousness, and rules would only get in the way. As long as it seemed reasonably unlikely that anyone would die, we were OK with it. And even if it seemed likely that someone would die, well, it would all depend on who it was.

We set about finding contestants, trying to explain to people what we were doing: *You can do anything you want. Yes, of course you can be a boy – or a girl, if you prefer. A snake is fine, no problem. No, it doesn't have to be actual swimwear, the round titles are meaningless, really, just a little joke. Oh, absolutely, nudity is fine! The chainsaw is fine, too – just try not to drop it on anyone, haha!*

The AIDS Alliance had been on the go for about ten years and they used their connections and goodwill to rope in some celebrity judges. We also somehow managed to persuade Marc Almond to perform, and Agnes Bernelle, the then seventy-three-year-old German-Irish cabaret legend, agreed to duet with him. And, for good measure, she decided to enter her dog as a contestant! (When I and some of the contestants appeared on *The Late Late Show*, to Gay Byrne's bemusement, I had Agnes's shaggy dog with me on a leash.)

The audience didn't know what to expect and they got the unexpected. I hosted the whole chaotic affair (as I would do for the next seventeen years) and attempted to keep it all together, which was difficult when there were 'Misses' struggling to stay standing under the weight of chicken wire and papier-mâché bulls' heads, and others were struggling to move (or breathe) in tightly wound plastic. There were lip-syncers and live singers and poetry and dancing and drunken falling and wet paint. There were highbrow references to Celtic mythology that went over the heads of the drunken audience, and there were blokes in bad wigs with balloons for tits. There was the dog wandering calmly through it all, and there was a naked guy on a motorbike. It was chaotic and magnificent and magnificently stupid – and it definitely wasn't boring.

On stage, the 'Medusa Crown of Thorns' was won by Miss Tress, a gold-painted straight girl in a corset with two spray-painted gay boys on leads, but the real drama was up in the balcony where the judges were seated. The show had started an hour late and the judges were kept happy with a constant stream of booze, which they drank as quickly as it arrived. At one boozy point towards the end of the show, one of the judges, a famously grumpy, multiple-Grammy-winning gentleman, drunkenly decided that one of the other judges, either the Oscar-winning actress or the bestselling author, had made some kind of inappropriate, possibly lesbian remark to his girlfriend. Needless to say, the two doughty women, themselves a little worse for wear, took great offence at the scurrilous suggestion and robustly defended themselves. Voices were raised, shoving was instigated, drink was spilled and 'fucks' were liberally thrown until the two women decided to storm out in umbrage. Unfortunately storming out also meant storming down the perilously steep, shiny new stairs of this shiny new building.

Stairs so new that they hadn't yet acquired the grit and grime of age that serves to grip the shoes of sturdy but booze-unsteady middle-aged women. The bestselling author was first to the stairs but she had taken no more than a couple of steps before she spun and fell backwards, and the only reason she isn't now fondly remembered as 'Bestselling Author Who Died When She Fell Down the Stairs at a Drag Pageant' is because our friend Tom, who had been tasked with minding them as they got drunker, was a couple of steps ahead of her and she landed on him, while the no-less drunk Oscar-winning actress tried to grab her and pull her back upright.

It was, we all agreed, the best night ever.

That first event made barely any money – it was well attended but not busy enough to record a profit after the costs were accounted for – and Dublin AIDS Alliance weren't interested in doing another the next year. It was probably also true that the board of the AIDS Alliance wasn't entirely sure they should be associating with us because this was around the time that GAG was becoming somewhat infamous and we were attracting lurid tabloid headlines.

We, though, wanted to do another. As far as we were concerned this had the potential to be the perfect event. It was everything we loved. It was stupid and nutty and open and creative and fun and diverse and welcoming and outrageous. It was loud and brash and unashamed and queer. And underneath all that it had heart because it actually meant something. In its own small way it was an attempt to redefine Irishness, to queerify Irishness. The Alternative Miss Ireland contest said you didn't have to be a GAA supporter to be Irish. You didn't have to go to mass on Sundays to be Irish. You didn't have to listen to Planxty, drink Guinness, watch *The Late Late Show* or remember Italia '90 with misty eyes to be Irish. You didn't have to be a nice cailín to be Irish; you could be a fabulous Queen Cailín and be Irish too. You could be any gender or none. You could paint your face and blow glitter out your arse. You could wear a bikini with a paddling pool for a hat and be Irish. Hell, you could be Polish and still be Irish. You could be the queerest queer in all of Queerdom and you could be as Irish as Peig Sayers.

We were determined that it needed to be a charity event, organised and produced on a volunteer basis, so that it kept its heart and audience/participant goodwill. We also knew it had to raise money for an HIV/AIDS organisation because it was so rooted in the gay community, and all of us had lost friends to the epidemic. After some persuasion, an organisation called Cairde, which supported people living with HIV, agreed to get involved, and over the next seventeen years the Alternative Miss Ireland raised hundreds of thousands of euro for a whole list of charities and organisations working with HIV/AIDS.

The next year, 1997, we moved the show to a new, bigger, venue, upped the production values a little, and the place was packed, with hundreds more queuing outside hoping to get in.

Earlier that year I had met a sharp-witted ball of energy called Declan Buckley. Late one night at a drunken house party he emerged from the kitchen in a tea-towel wig and had everyone howling with laughter at his drunken mime versions of Olympic gymnasts doing their floor routines. 'You,' I said, 'should enter the Alternative Miss Ireland.'

He entered as Shirley Temple Bar, a twelve-year-old Community Games gymnast from Dublin, with a smart mouth, pigtails and verruca socks. She tore the house down. She was hilarious and had the audience in the palm of her hand, and by the time she performed her belly-achingly funny gymnastics routine in the final round, there were twelve hundred people chanting her name at the top of their lungs and a star was born.

There was absolutely no doubt that Shirley was the unanimous and enthusiastically acclaimed winner that year but it was also memorable for the contestant who was carried on stage inside a massive ice coffin. The 'coffin' was kept in a freezer van in the car park outside the venue till it was needed. Then the queen, Miss Untitled As Yet, climbed inside, the lid was put in place, and four big body-builders carried her, with enormous wet difficulty, through the venue and onto the stage. The ice was extremely heavy, and awkward to carry, and the entombed queen's passage to the stage was slow and ponderous. By the time she struggled to burst dramatically through the lid, the half-naked queen was blue, wet, shivering and quite possibly hypothermic. She might not quite have managed to pull off her dramatic entrance but she did send the broken ice lid crashing onto the judges' table in sharp chunks. Then, as she (wo)manfully struggled through her number, the stage lights didn't just warm her up, they also accelerated the melting of her coffin, which flooded the judges' table with glitter-speckled slush.

It was the following year's judges, though, who were in real danger.

The 1998 Alternative Miss Ireland (AMI) was won by Miss Tampy Lilette, a country-and-western singer with 'female trouble'. Tampy was the creation of Katherine Lynch, who was then waiting tables in a late-night café with Shirley Temple Bar, but after winning the AMI she went on to become a popular 'drag queen' comedienne on the gay scene, and eventually a household name on TV. But it was that year's runner-up who almost managed to steal the show with a now legendary diva-worthy flash of theatrical petulance.

Veda Beaux Reves had entered and she had entered to win. When she was announced as the first runner-up, she took her bouquet of flowers, accepted the runner-up trophy – the Golden Briquette – and returned to her place in the lineup, but she was not happy. In fact, she was overtly pissed off. And as the crowd roared its approval on realising that Tampy Lilette must be the winner, Veda remained so. As Tampy's name was announced and she was adorned with the Medusa Crown of Shamrocks, then gave a short, tearful speech of thanks, Veda's demeanour remained unchanged. But one of Veda's many talents is knowing what people want and giving it to them right between the eyes. At that moment Veda knew what the room wanted – no, needed – was a diva, so she'd give them a fucking diva. She stepped forward out of the line and, with a flick of her glossy black mane and a surprisingly accurate aim, she launched her heavy bouquet and her Golden Briquette at the judges' table where they narrowly missed pop impresario and music mogul Louis Walsh, sending drinks and diving judges in every direction. For a split second the whole room stopped, before the capacity crowd bellowed its approval. Now, *that* queen knows how to put on a show!

Veda entered again the following year, and Louis Walsh, who had enjoyed himself thoroughly the year before, was back again as a judge. When it looked fairly sure that Veda was going to win, Louis, displaying the kind of knack for publicity that has kept him in the business and on *The X Factor* for so long, mischievously tried to persuade the other judges to give Veda the runner-up spot again. He just wanted to see what would happen. However, less mischievous heads prevailed and Veda was crowned the Alternative Miss Ireland 1999.

The next year the AMI picked up her skirts and moved into the faded Victorian grandeur of the Olympia Theatre, which would be her home for the next twelve years. Now we had a proper stage with bars to hang scenery from, sides to appear from, proper curtains and lots of dressing rooms, so the production values went up many notches. We were conscious of not losing the riotous club feel of the event so kept the bars open throughout, removed the seating in the stalls and had standing only on the ground floor. Every year thereafter, on the Sunday closest to St Patrick's Day, the gay community and its friends would celebrate their own queer version of Irishness. The whole 'heel-clickin', snake-banishin', roller-coastin' donkey ride' became colloquially known as 'Gay Christmas' and all day, while the production crew and the contestants were rigging lighting, hanging sets and teasing wigs, all around the city the audience were sewing on sequins, squeezing into hot pants, and having cocktail parties in preparation.

Backstage was always chaos! pandemonium! with up to a hundred and fifty performers and crew squeezing up and down the corridors and in and out of dressing rooms, wearing everything but (or on one memorable occasion including) the kitchen sink. It became a major production and every show might have thirty individual performances, each with its own sound, lighting and prop requirements, but as the years went by and every year the same amazing people volunteered to be involved, we learned how to pull it all together more and more efficiently till eventually it was a reasonably well-oiled machine, gliding along on hard work, goodwill, fun, vodka and a stern talking-to from Dizzy, the take-no-nonsense, clip-board-wielding drag queen who took over as producer after Trish decided to abandon us and have babies with a lovely man in Cork.

Over those years there wasn't a lot you can imagine that didn't at some point happen on that stage. Or fall off it. There was the time Miss Big Chief Random Chaos put an endoscope up her arse and the 'live' video feed showed it edging its way along his colon till it bumped into George W. Bush. There was Miss Heidi Konnt, the goose-stepping, leather-loving von Trapp babysitter, who won the crown in 2005 with a heart-warming song about fisting and poppers, accompanied by the von Trapp family in matching made-from-curtains outfits. There was the Edwardian lady Miss Mac Dermott, who refused to use modern conveniences, like electricity or amplification, which were not true to her era: she stood on her head and shouted at the audience through a tin cone. What she shouted was actually a rather beautiful contemplation on the human condition but nobody except me could hear her. There was the imposing, enormous, towering Miss Revvlon, seven feet tall in her stockinged feet (and even more towering in the platform boots she had made for herself out of cork tiles), introducing us all to his tiny Belfast mother in the audience. There was the bunch of straight boys in Speedos who shot their daredevil Miss out of a cannon and across the stage to the strains of Diana Ross singing 'I'm Coming Out'. There was the young overexcited queen who fell off the dangerously high stage into the pit and gave the venue management a collective heart attack. (The gays weren't fazed.) Miss Minnie Mélange, the little person who flipped the pantomime favourite *Snow White* on its head by playing Snow White while the 'dwarfs' were all average-sized, and her father, also a little person, was the handsome Prince. The drag king dressed as a giant chicken who still managed to channel Elvis Presley. The numerous nervous young queens who emerged blinking into the light in front of an audience of two thousand raucous punters, like young deer timidly emerging into a forest clearing, and promptly fell down the steps in their unfamiliar high heels with their genitals awkwardly taped between their ass cheeks.

During the contestants' performances I would sit onstage, on a sofa tucked to one side out of harm's way, microphone in hand, at the ready to jump in if something went horribly wrong or another nervous Miss came a cropper on a sequin carelessly shed by a previous Miss. Mostly, though, I would sit there drinking and cackling with Dizzy and Dolly, two seen-it-all-before, unimpressed queens in up-dos and diamanté, whose job was *supposed* to be helping queens and their props on and offstage but who kept me and half the audience amused by sneering with their eyes and doing their level best to sabotage most of the acts. Dolly would regularly lean across to me, drink in diamantéd hand, two rheumy eyes suspiciously regarding the 'arty' antics of whatever queen was on stage, and out of the side of her mouth she'd ask, with deliberation, 'What is this *shit*?'

According to a note I wrote on the back of the programme for the final AMI in 2012, we had seen in total over the years:

- *186 contestants*

- *634 performances*

- *79 judges*

- *4 venues*

- *21 hissy fits (4 spectacular, 2 legendary, and 1 that involved the police and two ambulances)*

- *2 snakes*

- *1 dog*

- *3 drug tests (1 inconclusive)*

- *4 genders (all inconclusive)*

- *1 lesbian punch-up*

- *1 lesbian make-up*

- *26 'Oh no she didn't!'*

- *1 'Oh yes she did!'*

- *3 apoplectic health-and-safety officers*

- *swollen genitals*

- *plenty of bruises*

- *lots of walkouts*

- *countless tears*

- *numerous boo-boos*

- *innumerable disasters*

- *myriad heart-warming moments*

- *1 accusation of Satanism*

- *1 police investigation and*

- *1 jam jar of human poo, which was never explained or returned to its rightful owner.*

Every year the contestants, their themes and performances reflected a changing Ireland and the concerns of the day. The year the scandal of abuse in the Church blew up, the show was a parade of blasphemy and channelled anger, with buggering priests, randy nuns and evil bishops. When the campaign to bring in civil-partnership laws was coming to a head, there were wedding dresses, stage divorces and anti-gay fundamentalists. As the economic boom continued, we started seeing contestants from Poland, Spain, Malaysia and the US, and for many years there was the winner of the Alternative Miss Philippines, a heat organised by the Filipino Nurses Network in Ireland.

In 2012, when she turned eighteen, the Alternative Miss Ireland was as popular as she ever had been, and we decided it was time she moved out of the house and got a job. Eighteen years is a long time to be doing anything and we were tired. It took up an enormous amount of time every year, and it was becoming harder for us, especially as core people from the AMI family had moved to other cities, other countries, or gone from being easygoing students to middle-aged people with careers, kids, businesses and lives.

Also, the pageant had always been about raising money for HIV/AIDS organisations, and over the years, as the nature of the epidemic changed and treatments improved, we saw these organisations change too, shift focus and, in some cases, cease to exist. The nature of the projects we were funding changed, too: they were less urgent. And there was something poetic about finishing on the eighteenth, and something right about ending it when it was still successful and enormously loved. Better to kill her off then than have her slowly die in another ten or fifteen years.

The AMI is gone, but I'm happy to say she's fondly remembered by all who sailed in her. And she left a legacy, visible in the vibrant Irish drag scene today. The Alternative Miss Ireland helped shine a light on, and give a platform to, a kind of performer that Ireland hadn't seen much of before and I'm proud of that.

12. A Big Disease With a Little Name

THINGS WERE GOING WELL FOR me in 1996. I was living with Niall and Frank, waiting tables for cash by day and running amok at night. I had no great plan, but I was only twenty-seven and happy yet to work it all out. I was young, I was invincible. I was in my prime.

One day in the spring I went to my doctor, nothing serious, just feeling a little unwell. He ran a few blood tests, nothing serious, just checking some stuff, routine. When the bloods came back he noticed my platelet count was low, nothing serious, could be all sorts of reasons. Still, he might as well do a full screen for everything, you know, just to rule stuff out. HIV infection is one possible explanation but one of many! He's sure there's nothing to worry about. But, you know, to be on the safe side and all that. He'll just do the HIV test. Put my mind at ease, right?

A few days later he called me. He told me he had the results and asked me to come in at the end of the day – which I *now* know is a bad sign. (He knows this might take time and could be messy so he doesn't want a waiting room of people outside.) It was a lovely warm sunny day, the kind of spring day that speaks of approaching summer and lifts your mood. I walked to his office near Grafton Street, the spring in my step, unconcerned. I'd come of age in the era of HIV, the panic, the scares and the ads on TV. Safe sex wasn't something I'd had to adjust to, it just *was*. It was second nature, just how things were.

My doctor is a nice man – cheerful, kind, thoughtful. A little tubby. I don't know much about his private life but he's a father, he likes motorbikes, and he told me I was going to die.

Of course that's not what he said, but that's what I heard, that's what I understood. What he actually said was that the test had come back positive for HIV.

For a fraction of a moment, an insta-second, I could see where I was with absolute clarity. I could see each item on his desk – the stapler, the notebook, the pen that lay askew against a desk calendar. I could sense the room around me, the closed door behind me, the chart on the wall. I could feel how much space I was taking up in the room, the air I had displaced from it with my infected body. And I could see the nice doctor sitting on his chair, facing me directly, leaning slightly forward – concerned, kind, uncomfortable. Waiting to see how I'd react, how bad it was going to be. I felt sorry for him.

He said something about a false positive being a possibility so they'd have to redo the test, but it was clear he didn't believe that for a moment. He started to explain some things but I wasn't really listening and didn't need to. I was a twenty-seven-year-old gay guy. I knew people who were sick, I knew people who had died, I'd been to AIDS funerals. I was under absolutely no illusions about what this meant. This was a death sentence. I was going to die. And it wasn't going to be a nice Hollywood passing away, it would be an ugly death. Gaunt and skin-marked. Without even the dignity of battle with a named disease, a proper noun I could rage at. I wouldn't be stoically battling cancer, or heroically grappling leukaemia, I'd be brought low by a vague syndrome. Hobbled by ridiculous, weird, old-timey afflictions, like tuberculosis, Kaposi's sarcoma, salmonella. It would be painful, slow, grasping and hidden. People would be afraid of me. Friends would talk of it quietly and carefully, away from prying ears. My family would be guarded but the neighbours would talk anyway. And sympathy would be shaded – because hadn't I brought this on myself?

The doctor made an appointment for me at the hospital and gave me a strong sedative so I would sleep that night. I walked out into the warm, bright afternoon. The streets were busy with office workers heading home and people nipping in and out of shops before they closed. I crossed Grafton Street, and as I passed a flower-seller who was trying to shift her last bunches with end-of-day prices, she smiled at me, recognising me as a familiar face. I wanted to tell her I was dying. I wanted to tell *everybody* I was dying. I wanted to stand there in the middle of the hurrying, sun-squinting crowd, and scream, 'I'M FUCKING DYING!' I was suddenly angry. Angry at these shoppers and homeward-bound workers. I was angry that they were going about their business as if everything was completely normal, acting like the world hadn't just been turned upside down. I was angry that they were worrying about missing the next bus, angry that they were wondering if it was too soon to text that guy, angry they weren't all stopped and trying to breathe or not breathe, cry or not cry, scream or not scream. I wanted to grab a passing woman and shake her. 'How can you be buying a fucking Marks & Spencer cottage pie when I'm fucking *dying*?'

But I didn't. I didn't make a scene. I'm too painfully middle class to make a scene. Instead I turned and walked the short distance to the flat, angry at the inappropriately lovely weather and praying I wouldn't meet anyone I knew. *I must look like a mess. What does my face look like? Am I crying? Do I look sick?* I wasn't sure I'd be able to fake a casual interaction. *What if someone stops me to say, 'Hi,' and I scream into their face, 'I HAVE FUCKING AIDS!'?*

Back at the flat I told Niall and Frank. They were under no illusions either. They'd lost friends. Plenty of them. We didn't say much. We made jokes and I laughed instead of screaming. That night in bed I didn't cry because the hypnotic the doctor had given me made everything impossible, except uncomfortable, disturbing dreams.

Soon I was spending a lot of time at the HIV clinic at St James's Hospital. It was always busy, full of sick, wary people trying to be invisible. Gays, drug addicts, haemophiliacs and prisoners handcuffed to prison officers accounted for almost everybody. The addicts brought their chaotic lives with them into the clinic. Heroin had released them from normal social protocols so they shouted conversations, argued and showed you their sores, and staff spent a lot of time managing them, looking for them, reminding them of appointments, gently chastising them. The haemophiliacs were mostly frail. They'd been infected early in the epidemic and these were the survivors. The prisoners sat between matter-of-fact officers, and sometimes the prisoner's mother, taking the opportunity of an unscheduled visit, would turn up with a plastic bag full of chocolate and small comforts and sit with her pale son, telling him all the news and fussing over him. And the gays, greeting each other or awkwardly avoiding eye contact, depending on their history.

And there were sick people. Dying people. Gaunt, tired-looking people. People being wheeled through to the ward. People who were there one week and not the next.

The staff were busy, hard-working, occasionally harassed, and determinedly cheerful in the face of it all, with occasional flashes of gallows humour.

On my first visit the doctor said she wanted to put me on medication. Exciting new drugs had recently been approved and a new treatment strategy known as 'hit early, hit hard' was being advocated in the US. After some discussion, I agreed to start taking drugs. Lots of them. Thirty pills a day, to be taken at various times, some with food, some without, some in neat capsules, some in huge, powdery, gag-inducing tablets, and all with side effects. This was an exciting time, she told me. Early results were promising. There was a lot to hope for. Then I was sent down the corridor to the social worker's office where she told me all the ways the state could help me die. I could get a blanket allowance, and a special dietary-needs allowance, and a heat allowance. And the dole, of course! Because I wouldn't be able to work much longer – I'd be much too busy being sick and dying. She touched my hand across the desk.

I felt like I'd been wrongly accused in a police lineup. I didn't recognise this person they were talking about. This sick person rattling with medication and Granny's pillbox. This person who was going to stop working, wrap himself in a blanket allowance and lie back on the conveyor belt that would trundle him inexorably towards a funeral. I couldn't believe that person was me. I felt fine! *I'm fine! There's been some kind of mistake!*

I went home with a carrier bag full of drugs and a long list of possible side effects.

Today people are afraid of HIV. In 1996, they were terrified. New treatments were beginning to make real progress but the average person on the street wasn't exactly *au fait* with cutting-edge HIV research so, to them, it was still terrifying, the stuff of lurid headlines and tragic Oscar-winning Tom Hanks performances. Despite that, I decided to be open about it, or at least not to hide it. Thankfully, I hadn't spent long in the closet, but it had been long enough for me to know that I didn't want to go back to hiding something, go back to being ashamed. In fact, my hand was forced by a practical acceptance that I have a big mouth. How could I possibly keep this from everyone when it was all I could think about?

I dreaded telling people who cared about me. I had decided immediately that I wouldn't tell my parents yet. Not till I had adjusted to it. Not till I understood exactly what was happening to me, how the treatment was progressing, what the prognosis was. Not till I understood everything about it and could answer all the questions. But I would have to tell friends, the people I hung out with every day, and I dreaded it. Not because it would upset them (it would) but because there would be *emotions*. And I don't like having to deal with emotions. Public displays of emotion, mine or anyone else's, make me uncomfortable. I don't know what to do, how to stop them. So I was grateful when most of my friends knew me well enough to react by making bad jokes in poor taste.

I was waiting tables in the Elephant & Castle restaurant in Temple Bar and I didn't want to stop – I needed the money – but I knew I might have to work a little less, or request awkward shifts to accommodate clinic visits or medication regimes, so I decided to tell the then owners. It would have been easy for them at that time to express sympathy but let me go – a lot of people would have been very uncomfortable with an HIV-positive waiter – but they didn't. They told me to take whatever time I needed and come back when I wanted. I've never forgotten that kindness.

For the next few years my life was lived around taking medications. There was a strict schedule to follow, pillboxes to be filled, tablets to be counted out, meals to be eaten or not eaten at the right times, with the right drugs. Strict adherence to the regimen was vital because HIV is a cunning little asshole. It replicates dizzyingly fast and mutates around drugs. A single drug will only work for a short time because HIV will find a way to shape-shift around it. The new treatments depended on attacking it with three of a new type of drug simultaneously because it can't mutate its way round three at once, but for it to work, the three drugs in your system needed to be kept at sufficiently high levels all the time, twenty-four hours a day. And not only was taking all these drugs, at the right times in the right ways every day, a logistical and practical nightmare, each drug also came with its own collection of side effects. Side effects that constantly reminded me that these were powerful drugs, powerful *poisons*, that I was shoving into my mouth at the proper intervals. So there was fatigue and joint pain and nausea and diarrhoea and rashes and days when you opened the fridge and saw the rows of pill bottles and you slid to the floor and cried while no one else was home.

It was exhausting because you could never take a break from it. HIV didn't take breaks. I couldn't even forget about it for longer than an hour or two because my watch would start beeping, reminding me to take whatever combination of pills and capsules and enormous retch-inducing tablets my schedule told me needed to be taken at exactly that moment. Taking drugs became my full-time job and I was working split shifts and weekends and bank holidays and evenings and even fucking Christmas. Happy Christmas, here's your turkey and poison.

For a long time after my diagnosis, I didn't feel attractive or sexy. I was always tired, always complaining about this side effect or that. And I felt tainted, marked as unfuckable. Scarlet-lettered. But in time, as my body adjusted to the constant bombardment, and as the clinic tried me on different combinations of drugs till we found one that was less brutal, life started to reassert itself. Hormones and lustiness will find a way when you're in your twenties, and one night I went home with someone. I knew him a little – we had mutual friends, he worked in a late-night café I would go to sometimes, and we ended up in bed in his small flat in town. We had safe sex, of course, but afterwards I lay there, my head about to explode, trying to work out what to do or not do. *Do I need to tell him? Should I have told him first? What*

*if he freaks out? Will it be worse if I say nothing and he finds
out afterwards? What if he hates me for it?*

I sat up in the bed and told him and cried embarrassing
tears. He didn't freak out, this almost-stranger whose
small room I had just filled with awkwardness. He was
calm and nice to me as I sat naked on the edge of his bed,
my head in my hands, embarrassed and sorry for myself.

It was a while before I tried that again.

How do you tell your parents you have HIV? How do
you tell them you have this almost mythically terrifying
virus? This AIDS. This 'condition', this 'syndrome'. (Oh,
for fuck sake, let me just call it a *disease*! No one dies of
a *condition*. People don't waste away from a *syndrome*.
A *syndrome* doesn't make you vomit up your insides
and your medication with them. A *condition* doesn't
make people hesitate to drink from your water bottle.
People don't whisper behind your back that you have a
syndrome. You can't fight a euphemism, you can't scream
at a wishy-washy *condition*, you can't rage at a medically
accurate *syndrome*. I want a vocabulary I can punch in
the stomach. I don't care what your *Lancet* says, what
your dictionary says: I have a fucking disease.)

So, how do you tell your parents you have this disease
that will turn the natural order of things on its head and
see them bury you?

I'd rather tell them a hundred times over I was gay than
tell them this. Telling my parents I was gay was difficult
and worrying, but in a way, it was out of my hands. It had

nothing to do with me. I didn't choose to be gay; I didn't decide to be gay. I didn't *want* to be gay – I simply *was* gay. When I told them I was gay I upended my parents' assumptions about my future. I forced them to adjust to a new, unfamiliar trajectory. I forced them to confront some of the things they'd always believed or been taught to believe, to re-evaluate previously easy moral judgements. And I had given them cause to worry: would I be happy, would I be lonely, would I be treated badly? But none of this was my fault. It simply *was*, and not telling them wasn't an option. Not telling them would have meant constantly lying to them by omission and would have meant keeping them at arm's length. Keeping them excluded from my life, distant. Not telling them would have meant turning my parents into acquaintances.

I felt no guilt for telling my parents I was gay, but this was different. I felt guilty that I was bringing this pain to them. Of course I hadn't chosen to be HIV positive either, but it wasn't an intrinsic, inevitable part of me. I might not have known when or how or whom, but somewhere along the way, young and foolish and sure of my invincibility and probably addled with alcohol or lust or love, I'd taken a risk. I'd made a decision (or, more likely, just not made a decision at all) that had landed me here, a guy full of drugs and 'a big disease with a little name'.

And it was hard not to absorb some of the stigma, the guilt, the shaming and the blaming around HIV. There was a *tone* around being HIV positive. A shifting of the eyes, a mumbled accusation, a hint of distaste. We modern lepers were at best stupid, at worst sinful. We weren't innocent victims, unfairly afflicted with cancer, cruelly singled out by motor neurone disease, randomly struck with vCJD. We had done something bad and this was our harsh reward. And you didn't have to look far to find people who said our reward wasn't just harsh but also justly deserved. People who said we had brought it on ourselves and were deserving of little or no sympathy. Unlike the innocent haemophiliacs we, the junkies and the gays, deserved AIDS. For the religiously minded, HIV was a divine punishment sent from God for our homosexual ways. For the less religious (but equally censorious) it was Nature's admonishment. Our comeuppance for 'unnatural' acts. The virus as moral agent. Conveniently, only HIV was a moral virus. Measles and yellow fever and all the others were just unfortunate because nice people got those too. But viruses aren't moral agents – if a virus found a way to survive by infecting people making their First Holy Communion, it would.

'What did you do?' and 'How could you have been so stupid?' were the accusatory questions hanging (usually) unspoken over people like me, and Ireland, of course, has a particularly rich history of blaming people for their sexual behaviour. A rich history of blame that ended up with forced adoptions, back-street abortions, ruined lives, and a terrified young woman dying a cold, lonely death in a grotto in an ordinary midlands town. A terrible history of shame that gave us mother-and-baby homes, Magdalene laundries and unmarked cemeteries. An architecture of shame.

Prudish and censorious, we hounded young women into institutions, with wagging fingers, pinched mouths and exasperated cries of 'Stupid girl!' For generations we asked incredulously, 'How could they have been so stupid when they knew full well the terrible consequences of winding up pregnant and unmarried?' while wilfully ignoring the fact that all they had done was what their very DNA urges them to do. They had done only what millennia upon millennia of evolution demands they do. They had done only what every living organism on the planet is born to do. What their hormones, their synapses, their serotonin, their blood and bones and cells are crying out for them to do. What their very biology insists they do.

The question isn't why so many young women had sex despite the awful consequences but why so many others didn't. We breathe because we have to, we eat because we have to, we drink because we have to, and we have sex because we have to. Our biology conspires to make us have sex, and it does so with bubbling hormones, powerful urges and a deep, human need for closeness and intimacy that at times overpowers us. Addles us. We stay with partners everyone else can see are bad for us, we make fools of ourselves over lovers that don't deserve us, we are swept away by passion and lose ourselves in skin and heat and sweat, and sometimes we can't resist our own biology and end up marked with other people's holier-than-thou shame.

So, I went home to Mayo, about a year after my diagnosis, and waited till my parents and I were alone in their living room, the TV on, no one really watching it. My mother's brown bread and half-pot of cooling tea on the little 'tea table' in the middle of the room, my dad making a *whooshing* sound as he pushed back in his recliner to raise the leg rest, my mother adjusting the angle of her head to bring the crossword clue into focus, a snuffling dog farting on the sofa beside me. It was ordinary and comfortable and nice.

'I have something I need to tell you.'

I had come prepared, with rehearsed simple explanations of treatments, drugs and terminology on the tip of my tongue: CD4 counts and viral loads and combination therapy. An upbeat and positive assessment of how my treatment was going, the great results I was seeing, and a determinedly optimistic and rose-tinted explanation of the wonderful new drugs and exciting new research. And my parents sat there and listened and, not for the first time in my life, they amazed me. My mother cried a little but they were calm and thoughtful and steady. They asked questions and kissed me and told me they loved me and went to bed, and I stayed on the sofa with the smelly dog and cried. I cried for the mess I was in, I cried for what I'd done to my parents, and I cried for how lucky I was to have them.

Sixteen years later *everything* has changed. I didn't know it at the time but I was lucky to be diagnosed when I was, on the very cusp of new, effective HIV treatments. I now have a chronic manageable *condition*. I take one small pill a day and I get on with my life. I visit the clinic a couple of times a year: they take some blood to check everything is still fine, I chat with the doctor, see if I can charm my way into a couple of sleeping tablets for a long flight I'll be taking soon, joke with one of the addicts about his swanky watch, and steal the nose off a little boy to keep him occupied while his mother is in getting her bloods done. I'm there so rarely now I don't know half the doctors any more and I struggle to remember my patient number. Even the clinic has changed, moved to a different building, the chaos replaced with an almost dull orderliness, appointments and small queues bum-shuffling along plastic chairs. The *weight* has gone out of the place. The heaviness of sickness has lifted, and death has gone back to other parts of the hospital.

The staff still work hard but now they complain about the ordinary annoyances of ordinary workdays: the roster, somebody's poor time-keeping, mixed-up labels. And no one tries to get you to apply for a blanket allowance.

Not that everything is perfect. There is still a lot of stigma around being HIV positive. Things may have changed dramatically when it comes to treatment, but people are still afraid. Even people who really should know better, like the gay community, are afraid. It makes dating difficult. Fraught. Sometimes hurtful. Everyone dates online now and it's common to see guys online describe themselves as 'clean' and say they are only interested in dating other 'clean' men. 'Clean' is a euphemism for HIV negative, and by implication, of course, HIV-positive people are 'unclean'. Many HIV-positive guys decide to bypass all that and only date other positive men.

I have settled on a three-date rule. If you tell him straight away, before he's had a chance to get to know you, the chances are he'll cut his losses and suddenly become really busy – too busy for that second date. But if you leave it too long, there's a good chance he'll be angry or upset that you didn't tell him sooner. So, I tell him on the third date and it's never easy. It's impossible to know how people will react. Some will bluntly say they can't handle that and you never see them again. Some will say it's fine, they understand, they have an HIV-positive friend, no problem, they'll call you tomorrow … and you never see them again. And some will pleasantly surprise you. Of course, when you are Panti and every gay in the country knows you, some say, 'I already knew. I was wondering when you'd tell me.'

When I was first diagnosed with HIV it was almost all I could think of. It filled my days, was inescapable. Now I rarely even think about it. In many ways it's like the small tattoo I got just by my shoulder when I was eighteen and tipsy. I can't see it and never think of it. I can go for six months and not even remember I have a tattoo until tattoos come up in conversation or someone mentions it when I take my shirt off at the beach, or catches sight of it when Panti is wearing a low-cut dress. And when it does come up in conversation I struggle to remember which side it's on. I don't think of myself as a tattooed person. It's a small part of me that doesn't impinge on my daily life.

Living with HIV now is similar. I don't think about it. I don't think of myself as *someone with HIV*. I'm not sick. I'm healthy and strong and expect to live as long as anyone else. I take my daily pill on autopilot, like I make my morning coffee or brush my teeth. I take that pill lightly, yet that pill is magic. It has returned me to life, to normal, ordinary, just-like-everybody-else life. It has even made me non-infectious, which, although it makes little practical difference, is psychologically important to me. When you have a communicable condition, an infectious disease, you feel marked, untouchable. Tainted. I don't feel like that any more. Even if I'm occasionally still treated like it.

That pill does something else for me. It removes people's pity. I always hated people's pity. The significant look you'd get when you told someone. I never wanted anyone's pity. I occasionally wanted understanding, compassion, even sympathy at times, but I never wanted pity. Pity takes the power away from the pitied, leaves them weak and defenceless, and I never felt powerless or defenceless. There were times when I felt tired, fed up, hard done by, angry, frustrated, sad, but never powerless. I always felt, despite all evidence to the contrary, that I'd be OK. That I was magic. And believing that *made* me OK.

I don't mean that I imagine I could have *believed* my way to health without treatment. I don't mean I think all you need to beat HIV is the power of positive thinking. You won't catch me reading *The Secret* or going to faith healers or growing my own wheatgrass. I'll take the drugs, thank you very much. But I refused to believe that that little asshole HIV was going to beat me, and that made me *feel* better. It helped me take the medications when they were hard to take. It helped me to continue taking them when I wanted to stop. It helped me to go to work and make plans. It helped me to go dancing and kiss boys and make AIDS jokes and laugh at this horrible thing. It took the power away from this crappy little virus and gave it back to me. I was *magic*. I always told the doctors, 'I'm magic,' and magic people don't get sick and die from a tiny fucking virus. Magic people survive.

And it turns out I was right. I *am* fucking magic.

13. Gender Discombobulation

I HAVE MANY THINGS TO thank the Alternative Miss Ireland for – many great friends, many great times – but one thing it gave me that I suspect I might never have got any other way was other drag queens. It gave me drag-queen friends to scheme with, and perform with, laugh, drink and fight with. Queens to borrow clothes from, compare makeup with, and discover new press-on nails with. To 'kiki' with. To be drag queens with.

The Alternative Miss Ireland was in large part responsible for ushering in a drag explosion in Ireland, for sowing the seeds of the vibrant and crowded drag scene we have in Dublin today.

Shirley Temple Bar, Veda, and Katherine Lynch were the first to take the opportunity presented by winning the Alternative Miss Ireland and parlay it into successful, lengthy careers by working their asses off.

All three developed their own long-running shows, and in turn gave opportunities to other queens (most of them also past AMI contestants) by having them on as guest performers. Soon other clubs wanted a drag show, PR agencies wanted queens to liven up events, and the drag scene started to blossom. Younger queens wanted to be a part of it and older queens who had done the odd show on an amateur basis were encouraged to take it more seriously. And soon that 'first wave' of queens was bringing up its own drag daughters and a second wave followed, with Davina Devine, Victoria Secret, April Showers, Imperia Queen of Spain, and then a third wave, and there was Bunny O'Hare and Regina George and Blathnaid McGee and Phil T. Gorgeous, then a fourth and a fifth, till nowadays you can't swing a nylon wig on Dame Street without taking out a bunch of baby drags.

My working life in drag had started more by accident than design. I fell through a career, simply going from one gig to the next, until eventually I didn't know any other way to make a living. I never *planned* to be a drag queen: I was just trying to have fun and pay my rent. I always imagined that the next gig would be my last and soon I'd have to get a 'proper' job.

Today, if you're a young gay boy with a Lady Gaga obsession and a show-off attitude, you look at people like me and Veda and Davina, and you see us having fun (and it's a drag queen's job always to look like she's having fun, whether she is or not!) and paying our bills

(*Mostly. OK, sometimes. Jeeze! You'll get it next week!*) and you think, I want to do that. I could do that. Being a drag queen has become a legitimate career choice! And a more and more popular one. And why wouldn't it? Younger drag queens get paid to do what younger gay boys have to pay to do: go out, get drunk, be the life and soul of the party, and make a fool of themselves. A lot of people think that sounds like the perfect job for them.

Of course, it's not as easy as it looks – nothing ever is. For one thing, the opportunities are limited. Even in the biggest city there are only so many gay clubs, so many cabarets, so many street corners, and in a small city like Dublin, it's even harder. And you'd better be a grafter because there will always be more jobs for computer programmers and checkout operators than for drag queens and when you *do* get them, they'll pay horribly and you'll spend most of those few euro on tights and lashes and a taxi home at three a.m. And there won't be a boss checking what time you started learning a new number or a manager looking over your shoulder making sure you're working on choreography or writing a few gags, so you'd better be a self-starter. And the few gigs there are you're going to have to earn because every other baby drag wants that gig too so you'd better be at least as good as them. And you'd better be able to get along with people and work with people because you're going to need to collaborate with people: with other queens on shows, choreography and numbers, with

DJs, venue managers and a bored sound man, who once worked with Blur and now he's standing there looking at you in some crappy basement club wondering where it all went wrong.

And you'd better be respectful and fun because the one thing you need most is a drag mother. A drag mother will pass on her wisdom and her makeup tips, show you how to get some volume in that wig, how to 'beat' your face, how to contour for bone structure, how and where to pad, how to stand to create shape, how to stack lashes, find shoes, apply nails, glue wigs, walk in heels, create cleavage, use a mic, land a joke, deal with hecklers, pee in a corset. She'll let you watch and learn, encourage you, give out to you, and give you gigs. A drag mother can open doors for you, but no queen is going to adopt you if you have an attitude. It's the cute, sweet puppies that get taken home from the rescue centre first.

And once a baby drag gets her large foot in the door she needs to work out what kind of queen she is, and that can take a while because there are all sorts of queens. There are comedy queens, lip-sync queens, singing queens, arty queens, clown queens, dancing queens, cabaret queens, music queens, ukulele-playing queens, 'end-of-the-pier' queens, DJ queens, and any other kind of queen you can imagine. There are queens who look utterly convincing as women and pride themselves on it, and there are queens who rub glitter into their moustache and wear Minnie Mouse ears. And there are good ones and bad ones and awful ones and mind-blowingly brilliant ones. Of course, the average punter hasn't seen many drag shows so they imagine that every drag queen is just like the one they saw that time they were on holiday in Lanzarote: crude jokes, a Dolly Parton lip-sync with balloon tits, and finish off with a chorus of 'I Am What I Am'. Now don't get me wrong! I can get on board with crude jokes, balloon tits and sending me and my sunburn home with a chorus of 'I Am What I Am', but the problem is when people imagine that that's *all* drag can be.

I was keenly aware of the limited perception of what a drag queen can be when I first started writing and performing 'legitimate' theatre shows and I knew some people were thinking, *Why would I go to the theatre to see a drag queen? I already saw one in Lanzarote.*

Most young queens first dress up – maybe for a laugh at Hallowe'en – because it looks fun (it is) but some discover something they hadn't expected: drag gets them attention. And it's *good* attention. For a lot of these effeminate gay boys, school was not a bed of roses. When other teenagers turned their attention on them it was usually unwanted and unwelcome and ended with a shove or a wallop or sniggers and pointing, and someone shouting, 'Fag!' However, the moment they put on a wig and a frock they become the centre of a different kind of attention. People take her picture, and cheer her on through her number, and even if she looks a mess, everyone says, 'Girl, you look fabulous!' And it changes her. Out of drag she's still the quiet, invisible gay boy, but in drag she's someone else entirely – behind the armour of the makeup she's sassy and funny and loud and fun, and she's the life and soul of the party.

Depending on their act, queens can be found everywhere from theatres to art galleries to corporate functions. Shirley Temple Bar and I once did a gig in the day ward of a geriatric hospital. We'd been asked to do it by a Filipino friend who was a nurse there, and felt we couldn't refuse. We did numbers in front of the TV (using a boom box for sound) to an audience of frail elderly folk with oxygen masks, dozing in wheelchairs and beds. Neither they nor we had any idea what was going on.

For the most part, the typical drag queen plies her trade in the noisy, well-lubricated environs of bars and nightclubs to patrons who may not have come to see the show *per se*: it's just an incidental part of their big night out. This means that, unlike most performers, the drag queen has to fight for their attention over the booze, the flirting, the banter and the gay dramas. In these circumstances, the drag queen needs to be bigger than other performers, grabbing your attention with her hair, her sequins, her high kicks, and the big *sound* cheaply afforded to her by the classic lip sync. It's all very well to pull out your harmonica at nine p.m. in front of an audience of harmonica enthusiasts who've come to hear you play, but if you're going to step onto a small stage at one a.m. in a crowded nightclub full of drunk gays, half of whom have no idea who you are and nearly all of whom are annoyed that your show is interrupting their bedroom-perfected routine to the new Beyoncé single, you'd better not pull out a harmonica or you'll be beaten to death with it. Even a few good jokes probably won't win over this crowd because invariably the sound will be terrible, half the club can't see the stage, and you're being lit by a slowly revolving disco ball. There are five hundred homosexuals full of Jägermeister and Red Bull and each one is looking at you with a raised eyebrow and a face that says, 'This better be good, Bitch,' and what you need is big hair and even bigger sound, but seeing as the club is only paying you in drink tickets and a beer-sodden fifty, you're hardly going to be turning up with a horn section. So, you turn up with your ~~cassette/cd/~~iPod with an up-tempo much-loved pop hit on it and you emote the crap out of it till the sweat is pouring down your waterproof face.

Of course, the lip-sync is a much-maligned and misunderstood form, and you'll sometimes hear people dismissively opine that 'anyone can do that', which you'll know is patently absurd if you've been to many amateur drag shows! Some of those girls never get the hang of it.

However, while the classic gay bar lip-sync will stand a queen in good stead and can keep her off the streets, it can also be limiting, and if a queen wants to progress she's going to have to diversify and develop other talents.

I was first drawn to the larger-than-life visual and theatrical elements of drag simply because they were colourful and fun. But, in a way, they also gave me permission to break out of the rigid rules of gender expression our culture imposes. We live in a culture where gender expression is so enthusiastically policed that most men wouldn't dream of wearing pink trousers and would be the subject of ridicule if they did. (Even though before the 1940s pink was considered a 'strong' masculine colour for boys and blue more appropriate for girls. Our current association of pink with all things 'girly' and feminine is entirely arbitrary and entirely modern.)

At its most surface level, drag is simply a theatrical device, a visual exaggeration or extravagance that amplifies the performer but, like most cultures, our culture decided that females would be the peacocks and gave them the tools to exaggerate their appearance theatrically – makeup, hairspray, sequins, heels, colourful costumes – while these things were frowned upon when employed by men and considered feminine, dandyish or foppish. Makeup covers flaws but, more importantly, it makes our eyes more prominent, our lashes more fluttery, our mouths more pouty, our brows more arched, our cheekbones sharper. And this serves to exaggerate and amplify our emotions. We become open books, with every fleeting feeling readable. Painted, we become emotional big screens, telegraphing the slightest batting of the lashes, the tiniest quiver of the lip. Ironically, many women think of their makeup as a mask they hide behind, when in fact it's the very opposite – it exposes you. And in our culture, emotions are women's preserve. Men are supposed to repress emotion at all costs, to slouch stoically, to not care, to remain cool, to never react. But this means that males tend to be visually boring in a theatrical setting – even heterosexual male performers often end up feminising their appearance in order to be more visually interesting: glam rock stars, Spandex-clad big-haired metal bands, hip-hop's fur-and-jewellery-dripping 'pimps'. Indeed, the very act of stage performing – the exaggerated facial expressions, the expansive gestures, the expression of emotion – is thought of as feminine and not the preserve of the stoic, expressionless male. Even our language constantly reinforces these notions. The word 'histrionic' (which means 'relating to actors' and also 'excessively emotional') is almost entirely used to describe women. When it is used to describe a man it is loaded with implied 'feminine' insult – he's acting like a woman, not like a real man.

But, of course, drag is about more than that – it plays with notions of gender and identity. It constantly asks questions about what gender is. Is gender just performed? Is it real at all? Does it matter? Does how we present our gender affect how others react to us? What exactly is the gender presented by the drag performer? Is it a third gender? A non-gender? In my own case I wouldn't describe what I do as 'female impersonation' (as some drag performers do, especially those who specialise in celebrity impersonation) because although I am using the signifiers of 'female' I am not actually trying to convince anyone I am female. I am presenting a character that is neither male nor female, neither one nor the other, but rather something else entirely. And there's power in being something else entirely.

Of course there's a clownish element too. The drag queen as caricature, as larger-than-life cartoon, as court jester, as colourful fool, who is allowed to say from behind her mask of lashes and powder, hair and corsetry, what the regular peasant would be beheaded for. She is allowed to speak to power and occasionally prick it with a sharpened stiletto. Even in small ways, I am allowed to say in drag things I could never get away with out of drag. As Panti I can rib an audience member about what they're wearing, or poke fun at their taste or home town in a way that would seem mean and rude coming from Rory in a shirt. But (almost) everyone understands the court-jester role played by the drag queen and, anyway, it's difficult to take offence from a cartoon. Just as Bugs Bunny is allowed to smash Elmer Fudd over the head with a frying pan, so the larger-than-life drag queen may wield the metaphorical skillet.

Yet even in our relatively relaxed times, drag remains one of the last great taboos – you are a traitor to your gender. Cross-dressing still retains the power to disturb and discombobulate. The seemingly simple act of a male putting on the designated apparel of a female remains remarkably powerful. In many cultures people who don't sit easily in one gender or the other are ascribed magical qualities, deriving their power from containing the spirit of both male and female. In primitive cultures the local witch doctor is often a little light in his loafers, and amplifies his feminine qualities with costume and paint. In Native American tribes male 'two-spirits' were respected (and sometimes feared) and were fundamental to tribal life. In India the *hijra* are marginalised, outcast and feared. Western culture would prefer us all to sit squarely in the gender box we were put into at birth and never budge, and even today, not doing so retains the power to upset people. Indeed, not sticking rigidly to our culture's arbitrary gender-specific rules of dressing and expressing yourself is to risk opprobrium, confusion, outrage and worse. It can be dangerous out there for people who don't play gender nice.

Once, a student who was studying fashion at the National College of Art and Design asked me and some other queens to model her handbags at the annual graduation show. We agreed, and it was a hoot. The audience of proud family members and assorted fashion types whooped and cheered as we pranced and bounced down the runway, a silly, outsized and colourful break from the parade of skinny, serious models. At the end of the show the students would present bouquets of flowers to their college tutors and asked us queens if we would do it on their behalf. However, the tutor to whom I was meant to give flowers didn't appear onstage when her name was called, so backstage, as the audience outside were gathering their coats and preparing to leave, the students asked me if I would go out into the auditorium and present the flowers to her at her seat. I said, 'Sure!' and tottered out to find her. She was a large woman in her fifties, wearing her grey hair in a bouffant, and a big purple kaftan. I teetered over to her, tapped her on the shoulder and beamed at her. 'These are for you!'

In front of all the proud parents, younger brothers and sisters of the students, she turned, looked at me proffering the flowers and screamed, 'FUCK OFF! I'M A FULL-BLOWN WOMAN AND I'VE NEVER BEEN SO INSULTED IN MY LIFE!'

Which, to be honest, seemed unlikely to me, considering her charming personality. Still, my mere presence was enough to set off in her an apoplexy of rage. Though this was a woman who was clearly very sensitive to gender issues, a fact that was belied by her own phrasing – using the language of disease to describe her own womanhood: 'I'm a *full-blown* woman', as if being a woman was akin to having AIDS.

Cross-dressing puts you on the lower rungs of the

social ladder. Interestingly, a man dressed as a woman stands lower down that ladder than a woman dressed as a man. That, of course, is *partly* because women have long appropriated many of the accoutrements of male dressing – trousers, jackets, suits – but also because they are still perceived to be the weaker sex. Therefore, in a weird way, a woman dressed as a man is somehow seen as having empowered herself, while a man dressed as a woman is somehow seen to have weakened or demeaned himself.

One effect of this, though, is that when people see me standing around in public dressed as a lady, they feel they can tell me anything because they are sure that I, in my frock and makeup, won't judge them (which shows how little they know about me!). Total strangers will come up to me in a bar and tell me the most intimate details of their lives. They'll tell me, a complete stranger, things they may never have told another soul because they are confident that I, the crazy drag queen, can't possibly judge them. They tell me all sorts of things: about the time they slept with their cousin, or peed themselves in the changing room in Arnotts, or when another girl fingered them on a school trip to Kenmare.

You learn a lot in drag.

14. Getting On With It

A S THE NEW MILLENNIUM PROGRESSED, Panti
continued to pay my bills. Countless thousands
of times I sat in front of a mirror and spent the
next two hours painting a new larger-than-life face onto
my ordinary workaday one. And in dressing rooms and
toilets, tents and hotel rooms, I wriggled into tights,
squeezed into corsets, clambered into shoes and ducked
into wigs before tottering onto stages and dance floors,
catwalks and sets. I did shows at clubs, gay bars, festivals
and Gay Prides up and down the country. I promoted my
own club nights and collaborated with other queens and
promoters. I wrote agony-aunt columns, emceed fashion
shows, hosted awards shows, did bit parts in TV shows
and small movies, and I annually hosted the Alternative
Miss Ireland and Dublin Pride. I broke heels and bruised
ribs and sweated and worked, and it was enjoyable for
a long time.

But as I moved through my thirties I was getting bored. I started to feel I needed to do other things, push myself. I was beginning to be frustrated that my 'career' – such as it chaotically was, if you could call it a 'career' at all – was stalled at this level. Noisy shows in noisy bars, the add-on entertainment. I knew I was capable of more than fun lip-syncs and a few gags. I wanted to say more, do more, communicate more, but I couldn't, hemmed in as I was by nightclub stages, twenty-minute sets, and the demands of Saturday-night revellers. Now, don't get me wrong! I love doing my club act. I can still lose myself in my favourite lip-syncs and there's nothing like the boisterous, electric energy of a late-night crowd and boozed-up hecklers, but I wanted to be able to do other things *too*. Subtler things, more nuanced things. I felt I was butting up against the outer limits of what was possible where I was, and I would have to move sideways first if I was to move on.

I already had a sense of where I wanted to go – I wanted to tell stories. My stories. I would be a storyteller, a drag *seanchaí*. It was an element of my club act anyway – stand-up, monologue – and years of emceeing events and making speeches at Prides and Alternative Miss Irelands had given me some kind of template. I had already done a small experiment in a fully spoken word show by writing an 'illustrated performance lecture' about the history of drag (which itself grew out of the opening monologues I used to do at Gristle, the early-evening cabaret before our H.A.M. club), which I performed a couple of times. It wasn't until I met Phillip McMahon, though, that Panti moved into the theatre.

Phillip is a theatre guy – he grew up in Dublin Youth Theatre and did a stint as an actor before becoming a playwright and one half of the production company *thisispopbaby* – but I met him through the clubbing scene. By then he already had a couple of plays under his belt and was emerging as one of a new breed of Irish playwrights influenced by club culture. So Phillip, equally at home in the theatre or a festival tent with a bunch of drag queens, wasn't frightened off by a glitter-and-grease-painted queen with a big mouth. Phillip thought, *Let's put her in a theatre*. He suggested we make a small show for the Dublin International Gay Theatre Festival: I would write it, he would direct it, and his production partner Jenny would produce it.

That first show was really an experiment. We would try some things, see what worked, what didn't, see how Panti best translated to the very different atmosphere of the theatre. *In These Shoes*, based around the women who had supposedly influenced Panti, was delivered in the form of a drag-school lesson and it ran at the tiny New Theatre in Temple Bar for a week. It was a small, gag-heavy, light show but it found an audience, was well received, and we ended up piling into a van and taking a road trip to Galway to do it there too.

In the seven years since, we've gone on to make

four more shows together – *All Dolled Up*, *A Woman In Progress*, *Restitched* and *High Heels In Low Places*. We've done fringe festivals and main festivals and ended up in the national theatre. We've carted a set across Australia twice, and watched with raised eyebrows as middle-aged middle-class ladies filled the seats in Paris. We've played in an inflatable theatre in Brighton and taken our stand-up show to Vicar Street. It's been an amazing, rewarding and exciting journey.

When you step onto a stage, alone, in a theatre, it's an intense experience. The audience is sitting in the dark, facing you, silent and expectant. They have paid to come and see you; they've taken cars and buses and trains, and now they're there, waiting. Waiting for you to entertain them, to enlighten them, to make them laugh or cry or think. Waiting for you to make them *feel*. You are in a crowded room and yet you are entirely alone, and for a moment you stand there, in the glare of the light, sensing the audience more than seeing them. You feel like you're in an empty roller-coaster car, poised at the very top of its arc, the adrenalin coursing through you as it tilts forward. Then you open your mouth to speak and the car rolls over the edge and the next ninety minutes is a blur as the car falls along the framework of the words you wrote and rehearsed.

In some ways it's terrifying, but in others, for someone who came from a nightclub background, it's liberating. When you're performing in a noisy club or a boozy cabaret the audience have distractions – there are drinks to be ordered, toilets to go to, friends to greet, boys to flirt with – so as a performer you compete with these distractions by being big and bold and loud. There is no room for subtlety. But in the theatre the audience is quiet and undistracted, and is expected to be. In the theatre the performer can be small; in the theatre you can whisper. In a nightclub a gesture needs to be big and broad, but in the theatre a tiny movement of a single finger can tell a story.

Back in 2007 when I wrote my first theatre show I wasn't only looking to make artistic changes. As I pushed past my mid-thirties, I started to consider my future because, thanks to my magic pill, I suddenly had one to consider. I had been working hard for all these years but I had nothing to show for it. All around me the Celtic Tiger (then in its last gasp, unbeknown to us) was flashing its cash, driving its fancy cars and counting its shares, and I had nothing, apart from a box full of wigs and a bag full of costume jewellery.

I lived in a crummy rented flat, I didn't own a car and I had no savings. I had spent fifteen years filling the venues and the pockets of club owners and promoters, yet the one time I enquired about getting a mortgage, the lady across the desk looked at me, a drag queen with no steady income and a life-threatening condition, and shook her head. I needed to make some changes.

There aren't many obvious options for a middle-aged drag queen, except to keep plugging away, keep taking those gigs, keep hustling. Then one day I was in a burger joint on Camden Street, being interviewed by a journalist for something or other, when the owner of the place came by. Jay Bourke was a well-known entrepreneur with a string of bars and restaurants all over the country. I knew him because he had originally owned the well-known Dublin bar The Front Lounge and had hired me to host a weekly show there. Seven years later, when we met in his burger place, I was still hosting it, but he would also have been familiar with various other clubs and events I was involved with, like H.A.M. and the Alternative Miss Ireland.

'How would you like to open a gay bar?' he said.

Jay and his business partner had owned a handsome corner bar on Capel Street for ten years. It had started out as a fashionable straight bar but struggled to find a crowd on the less fashionable northside. The Front Lounge had found success by slowly and organically becoming a gay bar, and so Jay had turned his Capel Street bar into a gay bar too, and for a few years it did fine. But eventually it struggled to hold onto the gays, and by the time I met Jay that afternoon it had been sitting empty and closed for months.

Opening your own place is one of the obvious, but daunting, options for an ageing drag queen. What did I know about running a bar? Oh, I had spent my working life in bars and clubs but what did I know about the everyday mechanics of running one? About beer taps and gas and kegs and deliveries? Nothing. What did I know about the business or legal end of it, our arcane licensing laws? Nothing. And where the fuck would I get the money to invest in a bar? From nobody in their right mind, that's who.

But I could get a manager who knew about beer taps and deliveries, and I could learn. I'd partner with Jay and he could look after the licensing applications and the 'late-night exemptions'. And the money? Well, it turned out that nobody in their right minds was in charge of the banks in 2007. So all I'd need to do was get people in the door and the Lord knows I'd been doing that for long enough, except now it'd be my door. And so, after much discussion with friends and my father, I became a pub landlady.

The first job was to find a manager, someone who knew what he was doing. I asked around, and someone suggested a restaurant manager called Shane Harte. And I remembered sitting on the edge of his bed ten years earlier, my head in my hands, crying because I'd just told him I was HIV positive.

Sometimes I'm accused of having talents. That I'm a good speaker, or a good performer, maybe not a terrible writer. But I think my real talent is in finding good people to work with, then letting them do what they're good at. I put my image in Niall's hands, my shows in Phillip's hands and I put my bar in Shane's hands. Because my name is above the door I'm often given credit for everything good about Pantibar, but it's really Shane who deserves most of the credit.

Opening a business is exciting and exhausting, and for the first two years Shane and I spent almost every minute of every day at Pantibar. We painted walls and fixed pumps and ripped out bars, and I learned to change kegs, cash up and pull pints. It wasn't easy. Six months after we opened in November 2007, the economy imploded, people stopped going out, and over the next couple of years half our customers emigrated. And although we were only fifty metres from the river, we were fifty metres from the *wrong side* of the river. The river was a psychological barrier to the gays who were comfortable in their south-of-the-river gay triangle and it took us years to make them comfortable crossing the invisible north/south divide.

We struggled to survive and, on a couple of occasions, came within a hair's breadth of closing, but we worked our asses off and kept changing things and trying new things. We did open-mic nights and 'bear' nights and club nights in the basement. We did craft nights and live music events and comedy nights and movie nights. We did Eurovision parties and quiet afternoon pints, and wrangled with the neighbours about late nights.

We decorated and redecorated and decorated again. We had break-ins and floods, and one day the 'head shop' across the road was set fire to and three buildings went up in flames. It was exciting and exhausting and frustrating and worrying. And we survived and eventually thrived, and now, seven years later, Pantibar is stronger than ever. Most of the staff have now been with us for years and are like family. They work hard and play hard, and send pictures home to their mothers in Brazil of the giant drag queen they work for. I do my silly bar show there every Saturday, but now it runs so smoothly and the staff are so great I can tour my theatre show in Australia for a month, or take time out to write a book, and know that everything is under control.

15. Panti Politics

I SOMETIMES WONDER WHO I might have been had I been heterosexual. What kind of person might I have turned out to be, had I not been flaming? I suspect I might not like me very much. Perhaps that's unfair on Straight Me, but there's no doubt that all the conditions would have been there for Straight Me to be a jerk.

Straight Me would have been dangerously comfortable in the world. Born into a nice middle-class family, never spoiled but never without, smart enough (and encouraged enough) to do well in school and go to university, and afterwards a good job in a good company almost by birthright. Not a model, but decent-looking, healthy, good at football, with nothing to put me in the firing line of schoolyard taunts or adult discomfort – no disability, no speech impediment, no fatness, no buck teeth or gammy eye. I'd have the right accent, the right qualifications and the right genitals to be taken seriously by the world.

I would speak and people would listen. I would be fully participant in the world because the world was built for me by people like me. I would vote in elections because my opinion was important, and I would vote not to change things but to keep them the same. Why wouldn't I? The world would have been perfect already, and I perfectly comfortable in it. And Perfectly Comfortable Straight Me would have had no ability – and maybe no inclination – to understand or empathise with people who weren't so comfortable in a world that hadn't been built for them.

Yes, I know, I'm being unfair on Straight Me because he would have been raised by the same decent parents, had the same Traveller neighbours, the same trips with Dad to the home for the mentally disabled, his pockets full of Milky Moos to share, but still ... I can't help but wonder if I'd have turned out to be a dick.

Most of the things I like about me are rooted in my difference. I like the fact that I like the misfits and the oddballs and the freaks. I like that I like the fey fella who marches down Capel Street wearing a Panama hat, long silk scarves, pastel slacks with homemade piping made of ribbon up the side, and medals pinned to his chest. Even as a kid I didn't want to flick spit balls onto the back of the witch who lived in the funny little house with the dark windows you couldn't see in on the way home from school. I wanted to go home with her and learn to make potions. I like the fact that I'm not threatened by people who are different. I like the fact that I have Chinese neighbours, that my local Italian restaurant is staffed by Filipinas, and that there's a mosque on my street that spills handsome men onto the pavement on Fridays. And I like the fact that I'm willing to imagine that the way things have always been is not necessarily the best way.

I like the fact that, for a change, one Sunday ten-year-old me went to the Protestant church instead, just to see what their mass was like, and the small group of mostly elderly ladies wondered where this strange child had come from while I stood with my hands behind my back and smiled at them and decided it smelt different from our church.

And when I was old enough to understand what it was that was different about me, old enough to understand my gayness, it liberated me from assumptions. My gayness made me question everything around me, everything I'd been told, everything I'd taken for granted, because if everything I'd ever been told about being gay had been wrong – and it had – then couldn't everything else I'd ever been told be wrong? Being gay made me think.

And the underground gay Clubland I discovered was populated by people just like me. People who'd rejected everything they'd been expected to take for granted, and who'd found a place full of people just like them, where the rules were vague, made up as they went along, where creativity and outrageous investigation were prized above all else, where even gender was up for grabs. A place with its own secret codes, full of people who'd thrown off everything to be there, and now that they were, they were doing it their way, with disco and hanky codes, with poppers and sidelong glances.

When I found this world I exploded, and in its heady atmosphere of sex and colour, creativity and fun I continued to question everything I'd ever been told. I threw myself into its every dark and exciting corner. I revelled in the lights, the music, the smoke, the fun and the sex. And every sex act was a liberation, another push to question everything, to accept nothing as given, to assume everything is unproven till I'd worked it out for myself. I was young and gay and free, proving to myself, and the world, that everything you'd ever told me about sex and my sexuality was bullshit! 'Fuck you and your Popemobile!' I was saying to the world every time I got fucked.

My gayness had propelled me into this exciting new world and it was my gayness that gave me the freedom and the courage to make up my own mind about everything. And I did. We did. Being gay pushed us to think, and from it came a maelstrom of creativity, art, politics and passion. A lust for life and all it could be.

And I wouldn't change a single thing about it, because I was forged in that chaotic world and it made me the person I am today.

But in 2008 I didn't recognise the new gay world that had started to develop around me. Gay culture was changing and most of the younger gays seemed more interested in gym membership and fancy cocktails than changing the world. I had just turned forty and felt I should be putting my feet up in a world I had done my tiny bit to create, but instead my world was disappearing, leaving me stranded, cast away. I was a relic of a disappearing world. A fucking dinosaur. Granted, I was a bloody gorgeous dinosaur, but I wasn't meant to be a dinosaur!

Being gay had saved me, but this New Gay was killing me.

Because the New Gay was the opposite of creativity, the opposite of passion. It was an inoffensive, sickly sweet candyfloss of blandness created by corporations and devoured by thoughtless youth.

The gay culture that had rescued me was being replaced by a culture that questioned nothing. The New Gay didn't question, didn't search – Google did that. It had the whole world at its mouse tips but it only clicked on Hannah bloody Montana. Fifteen-year-old me, starved of anything that reflected me, read and re-read the section on homosexuality in Desmond Morris's *The Naked Ape*, thrilling at the clinical descriptions of sex acts, excited by the (mostly) non-judgemental tone, clutching at the hard evidence of a gay world somewhere 'out there'. But in 2008, any fourteen-year-old could watch Brazilian boys fucking each other before reading all about Stephen Gately's painful break-up in *Heat* magazine.

The New Gay hadn't struggled and fought to forge a hard-won identity, whose value it then appreciated. It hadn't searched to find 'the gay': bits of 'the gay' had seeped into its world. Corporate-friendly, sexually neutered bits. *Will & Grace* was on at teatime, and every evening de-sexualised gay men were beamed into your living room as they decorated your dreary houses or refurbished your middle-aged women. Your best friend and eunuch. Your granny knew where The George was, and young gay boys in Mayo could join online discussions about what the mean doorman said to whom last night, and why the DJ refused to play Miley Cyrus.

The underground had come overground, then shrivelled and died in the light.

Being gay had been emasculated. It was no longer a rejection of the status quo, it was embracing the status quo and adding a few cushions. Being gay was no longer dangerous and exciting and anti-establishment and mother-horrifying. It was easy and inoffensive and emasculated, and brought its mother to gay bars 'cos she'd love them.

But your mother shouldn't love them! When you're gay and twenty (Hell! When you're straight and twenty!), your mother should be horrified at everything you do. If she even suspects a small portion of what you're up to, she should be pulling her hair out in despair, frantic with worry, gnashing her teeth and beating her breast, howling with rage and praying for the courage to disown you.

The New Gay had jumped backwards over my generation. It was sitting on the sofa with its granny, tut-tutting at cruising and bathhouses and casual sex.

What was liberating and full of honesty to me was sad and shameful to them. The New Gay wanted to bring a boyfriend home at Christmas. I wanted to fuck Christmas!

The New Gay, raised at the comfortable teat of the Celtic Tiger (which was then imploding around them), wanted to go to sexless, shiny, over-decorated bars owned by straight corporations, and drink Bacardi Breezers on glass tabletops. I wanted to smash the glass tabletops and fuck on the shards.

Gay culture was being stripped of everything that made it interesting, dangerous and offensive. Plucked, emasculated and disembowelled. Shaved and polished, infantilised till it was a neutered, sexless child of indeterminate gender. Even the New Gay's icons were children's entertainers: Steps, Miley Cyrus, Britney. Entertainments designed for children filling dance floors in gay clubs.

I thrilled to stars like Morrissey, Boy George and young Madonna – stars who kicked against everything. But in 2008 the gays worshipped sixteen-year-old Christian Miley Cyrus. Instead of liberating you from a rigid world, being gay now gave you a new set of rules designed for children – packaged, anodyne, domestic. Britney was carrying around children and twittering about watching *Nemo*. Debbie Harry didn't have kids – she had sex. Our Madonna was wild and lascivious, shoving two fingers up to my mother, taking off her clothes and giving blowjobs in sex books. Their Madonna wrote children's books and adopted babies.

Domesticity was the New Gay and that wasn't the gay I'd signed up for.

The New Gay even rejected being gay! It wanted to be 'straight-acting'. It screamed, *'I'm not a gay man, I'm a man who happens to be gay!'* as if its sexuality was nothing more than a haircut. Something to be glossed over, rather than an intrinsic, integral and powerful part of you that colours everything you do and are. It rejected it as an identity because assimilation, not revolution, was the New Gay's dreary goal.

My generation was the generation who came of age under the shadow of AIDS. We grew up with sex and death inexorably linked. AIDS was there to kill us for going against Nature, to punish us for our promiscuity. And we adapted. We had ourselves tested, and watched friends die, but we never turned against sex and the liberation it had brought us. Sex defined us – and why not? Sex defines us all. Straight people just don't notice it so much, because their sexuality is simply part of the background, assimilated into every nook and cranny of everyday life. It's less obvious because it's ubiquitous. It's only gay sexuality that's thrown into relief against the heterosexual background.

Our sexuality awakened us, and sex itself was the physical, emotional and even political expression of our sexuality and ourselves. So we never, despite the horrors of the AIDS epidemic, gave up on sex. It was odd that it was the New Gay, those who had grown up post-AIDS, who had never seen friends die, who hadn't grown up with condoms and headstones on TV, who had given up on sex.

Being gay used to mean being part of a fire of creativity and exploration, but rather than burning bigger and brighter, in 2008 it seemed that the fire had dwindled to a barely smouldering ember.

But I had underestimated the younger gays. I was the old fogey on the bus, tutting at the youngsters and tarring them all with the same brush. I was shaking my fist and shouting, 'Get off my gay lawn!' at these feckless layabouts, when it turned out they were neither.

In 2008, the campaign for same-sex marriage hadn't yet caught the public imagination in Ireland, but neither had it yet caught the imagination of the younger LGBT community. They were too young and having too much fun to be worrying about grown-up stuff like marriage rights. Nevertheless, established, experienced LGBT rights organisations were working hard in meeting rooms and politicians' offices to get civil-partnership legislation through the Dáil. That was their priority, and once that was achieved, they'd work towards full marriage equality. But tensions were emerging in the community over this strategy.

A younger breed of activist was emerging, inspired and influenced, via the internet, by marriage-equality campaigns and successes in other parts of the world, and they were impatient and radical. The older activists knew that handshakes, lobbying and gentle nudging had got them to the brink of civil-partnership legislation, a stepping stone from the finish line, but the new, younger, activists saw civil partnership as second best, a cop-out. Some even felt it was an insult. They were fired up on viral videos and influenced by direct-action groups, like Act Up, which had achieved great success in turning the AIDS debate around in the eighties through creative, headline-grabbing protests. Now these younger activists were beginning to organise demonstrations, holding 'kiss-ins' outside the Dáil, and chaining themselves to railings. Some in the gay community were worried about this development, worried that the whole project could be derailed if nervous politicians thought the LGBT community weren't united behind civil partnership. Why take the political risk of alienating conservative voters if some of the gays weren't going to thank you for it either?

But I was excited to see it. I was excited to see a flash of anger, a take-to-the-streets energy from young gay people. Nothing energises me more than the sight of a dyke with a megaphone agitating on the streets! And, as far as I was concerned, it could only help, the more the merrier. So what if the two 'sides' weren't exactly on message? The general thrust of their arguments was the same: a thrust towards equality.

I was somewhat ambivalent about the drive for same-sex marriage. It seemed a very conservative project to me. One of the things I had always loved most about being gay was that it freed you from many of the usual dull pressures your straight friends faced. The pressure to find a nice wife, a steady job and a semi-detached in the suburbs where you could raise your steady kids. We gays were spared the inquisitive eyebrows of visiting aunts at Christmas, the gently probing questions of a mother with grandkids on her mind. Once you were gay you didn't have to care about football and you didn't have to bring home a fertile nurse from a nice family. The gays were free to work out their own ways to be happy, to form other kinds of relationships, create their own kinds of families.

I recognised that most of the LGBT community didn't share my ambivalence. They wanted the same things as their straight brothers and sisters wanted. They wanted the same respect as their straight brothers and sisters expected. And they wanted their relationships to be cherished equally. They wanted to be able to declare publicly, like everyone else could, the special status of the bond they shared with their partner, and they wanted that bond to be acknowledged and respected in the same way. They wanted simply to be able to say, 'This is my husband', 'This is my wife'. They grew up in a society that presents marriage as the goal. A society that encourages and urges them to get married. A society that raises them from the day they are born to be married. Fairytales always end happily ever after in confetti. Mammy smiles wistfully about her wedding dress and Granny remembers your mother's lovely cake – 'Four tiers!' Wedding anniversaries are celebrated, and isn't it wonderful to see the O'Reillys? 'Seventy-five years married they are!' Unmarried middle-aged women are embarrassed to admit it and unmarried middle-aged men are viewed with suspicion. But the day a gay person comes out they're expected to forget all that. Lesbian little girls grow up wanting to be princess brides too, but the day they came out as lesbian all that was whisked away: 'No, sorry, not for you! That's for your sister.'

So, despite my own ambivalence about marriage generally, I saw it simply as a question of equality. If gay couples wanted to get married, let them. Gay people have exactly the same hopes and dreams and ambitions for their lives as everyone else and should have the same opportunities as everyone else to fulfil them. We are full and equal citizens of this country and should be afforded the same rights and responsibilities.

I understood, too, of course, that there were many urgent and practical reasons why gay couples' relationships needed to be recognised equally under the law: inheritance rights, medical responsibility, taxes, bereavement ... Gay couples lived in a legal limbo where loving partners, who had committed their lives to each other, were treated as strangers under the law. And gay couples had children. Children they fed and clothed, loved and picked up from school. Children whose hair they brushed, sandwiches they made, homework they helped with. Children they cheered at the school sports day, worried over during exam time, and for whom they lay awake in bed waiting to hear them home safe from the disco. Children to whom, in the eyes of the law, they weren't related at all.

One Saturday afternoon in the spring of 2009, I got my dog and wandered into town to attend a marriage-equality protest organised by a new, youthful, energetic campaign group. The turnout was disappointing and it annoyed me. Where was everyone? Could the New Gay not tear himself away from his dating app for an hour? At the time I kept a lively blog on the Pantibar website so the next day, still annoyed, I wrote a blog post to get it off my chest.

NO MORE MISTER NICE GAY
Lazy-arsed queers

On Saturday afternoon, Penny and I went to the 'LGBT Noise' demonstration on Dame Street to support their campaign for gay marriage (and against the weak, second-class civil-partnership bill that is due to come before the Dáil – though I wouldn't hold your breath). There were about a hundred and fifty people there, mostly the usual suspects, and we had a pleasant, social afternoon.

Long-time activist Tonie Walsh made a rousing speech (delightfully, he couldn't resist aiming a few kicks at the Catholic Church. I howled when he referred to the Pope as 'that German eunuch in Rome'!) and Penny got lots of attention and met a few other gay dogs. It was nice to see some politically engaged young gays, and those of us who were there had our batteries recharged somewhat. And I think Noise were happy with the turnout as it was a lot more than their last demonstration at the Dáil.

But one hundred and fifty people? That's pathetic. There were a couple of thousand gays drinking and dancing and hitting on Brazilians within a five-hundred-yard radius of Dame Street twelve hours earlier. Where the fuck were they? Where the fuck is the righteous anger?

When some bouncer in The George is mean to a drunk gay, the forums light up with horrified nellies, protests are mooted, and Facebook groups are set up. But when a fundamental human right, available to everyone in every civilisation since the formation of human societies, is denied them, they can't be arsed getting out of bed. Where is the righteous anger?

When Sunday clubbing hours are curtailed, angry gays join angry protests outside the Dáil, petitions clog up our inboxes, and outraged gays shout about the nanny state. But when the government that taxes them the same as everyone else tells them that in return they'll only have some of the same rights afforded to everyone else, they can't be arsed having brunch an hour later than usual. Where the fuck is the anger?

When Alexandra and a bunch of other people you'd never heard of a few weeks earlier make it to *The X Factor* final, you won't leave the house and no one can get through to you because you're furiously text-voting, but when you're told you're a second-class citizen and your relationships aren't real relationships, you can't be arsed walking over to Dame Street from H&M because the cute assistant has just gone to check if they have that cute jacket in your size. Where the FUCK is your righteous anger?

And don't bother telling me that you're not interested in marriage. That you think it's an outmoded institution, a hangover from a patriarchal society that was only about the protection of property. I don't give a crap. Plenty of other gays do want to get married, and you should be furious on their behalf. Furious that something as basic and fundamental as marriage, something that is taken for granted by everyone else, something that society expects, encourages and cherishes for everyone else, is closed off to them, and them only. Anyone else can get married. Any race, any creed, any gender ... Hell! Any idiot, murderer, rapist, child molester. Any asshole, racist, queer-basher. Any dumb-fuck soccer hooligan. Any mentally disturbed lunatic. But not the gays! The sky will fall down!

And where were those gays who do want to get married? The ones who'll be rushing to the registry office if and when the weak-brewed, watered-down, domestic partnership version of marriage is thrown at us to shut us up, and the government slaps itself on the back for being modern and progressive.

Why the fuck are you watching your *Sex and the City* box-set when you should be rioting in the streets?

What is it going to take to make you angry? What is the spark that will finally light a fire under you? Are you waiting for a gay Rosa Parks? Well, you have one. In fact, you have two. Katherine Zappone and Ann Louise Gilligan have already refused to sit at the back of the bus. Do you need a gay Emmeline Pankhurst to throw herself under the King's horse? Will that finally wake you up? If you think the fact that you can hold hands with your boyfriend in Topshop is progress enough, then that's all you're going to get. If you act like a second-class citizen, you'll be treated like one.

And it's not just the gays I'm pissed off with.

I'm pissed off with the pensioners. When their medical cards were threatened, the streets were in tumult with anger. And rightly so. But the slight against the pensioners was much less than the one against us. The government wanted wealthy pensioners, who could afford it, to pay for their medical expenses, not deny them all a fundamental right given to everyone else. Can you imagine the reaction if the government had decided that pensioners' marriages were no longer valid? Or even if their marriages were to be downgraded to a weaker version of marriage, a faux-marriage, because, after all, old people's relationships aren't real, they're just pretend relationships so a pretend marriage should be good enough for them? They would have torched the Dáil.

And the pensioners didn't protest alone. Gay people were out on the streets. Gay people wrote to newspapers. Gay people lobbied their TDs, called radio shows, threatened to oust the government at the earliest opportunity. But where are the old folk when we need them? Why isn't your granny calling Joe Duffy to express her outrage that you are expected to take on all the responsibilities of citizenship but only some of the rights? And don't tell me she has a religious objection! I don't give a toss if she has a religious objection. She's welcome to it! We're not asking to get married in her church. We're asking – demanding – the right to civil marriage, under the same law, in the same state, that we, too, are supposedly equal citizens of. It's payback time, Granny. Quid pro quo.

And where are the bloody students? When college fees were mooted, gay people rallied, too. We scratched their back, and now they can bloody well scratch ours. Quid pro quo. And the farmers? Quid pro quo. And the unions! Where are the bloody unions? Gay people pay union fees too. And the nurses, and the teachers, and the rest. In the eighties, the Dunnes Stores workers went on strike rather than handle oranges that came from apartheid South Africa, a country and a people half a world away. And yet they couldn't give a toss that the guy working on the checkout beside them is segregated.

But it's hard to see why they should care when you don't seem to.

Perhaps the problem is that we gays have wanted to be left alone for so long that we're used to keeping our heads down. We don't like to draw attention to ourselves by rocking the boat. Well, I'm fed up not rocking the boat. It's my bloody boat too! I want to scream and shout and kick and throw things. I want to riot! I want to take to the streets and hurl abuse. I want people to know how pissed off I am. I want to break things and tell the people who campaign to keep us in our place to fuck off. I want to scream, 'How DARE you? How fucking dare you stick your nose into my business? How dare you try to tell me whom I can and cannot marry? How dare you tell me that my relationships aren't real? How fucking dare you? Fuck off and mind your own bloody business, you interfering, mean-spirited, petty, backward, ignorant, patronising asshole!'

I have a lot of respect for NOISE and their campaign. At least they're doing something. But I think the time for protests that are about making pretty pictures that will hopefully make it into the *Evening Herald* is over. What we need is righteous anger. What we need is a Stonewall riot. Oh, I'm not suggesting we rip up the pavement slabs and loot Arnotts. But what we need is a thousand gays to get angry on the street. What we need is two thousand gays with eggs to turn up at the Leinster House railings at Merrion Square and have them hail down on the cars of country TDs, to chain the gates shut, to refuse to move, to pour paint on the pavements. What we need is for fifty gays to get arrested. So what if we get arrested? A day in court and a fine? We'll have a whip round! But we need to get angry. We need to be our own spark.

No more Mister Nice Gay.

And a funny thing happened. I hit a gay nerve. The blog post went viral, was passed around and became the subject of debate in the gay community. It sparked online discussions, articles in newspapers and conversations in pubs. Not everyone agreed with me, of course, but many did, and suddenly it turned out that the younger gay community *was* interested in marriage equality. They were passionate about it. It wasn't my blog post that made them passionate about it, they always had been, but before this they didn't know how to contribute.

What did they know about politicians and conferences and meeting rooms? They didn't even own a suit. But here was that big drag queen talking a language they understood, about a campaigning organisation that spoke their language too, the language of Facebook posts and noisy demonstrations, and that was something they could contribute to. The debate sparked by the blog encouraged them to get up and get involved. It prodded them to agitate against the status quo, and suddenly the New Gay I'd been so hard on started to look more like the Old Gay I recognised. And at the next demonstration there were many more people, many more young people with placards, chants and whistles. And at the one after that there were even more, until eventually there were thousands and thousands of people marching to the Dáil.

I'm not saying my angry blog post was responsible for that, but it did play a role in lighting a fire under a section of the LGBT community that was waiting for a spark. And it was the first time I realised I had a voice. An effective voice. The gay community knew me. They knew me well. For years I'd been spinning on their stages, organising their parties, hosting their events, writing in their magazines and making speeches at their Prides. They knew who I was and where I'd come from. It's hard to ignore a drag queen anyway, but twenty years of sequins and sweat had given me a profile that amplified what I had to say. Drag, I learned, didn't muffle my voice. It amplified it – and that was a lesson that would stand me in good stead some years later when I was asked to address the audience in the Abbey Theatre.

It was also a lesson that was reinforced only a few months later. That June, Dublin Pride was invigorated by the campaigns for civil partnership (which would come to fruition the next year) and same-sex marriage, and by the tensions that had arisen in the community over them. As I usually did, I emceed the post-parade event in the park behind Dublin City Council's offices, an event that is part political rally, part party, with a mixture of speeches and entertainment. It was a beautiful sunny day, and during my own address to the colourful crowd, I tried to ease some of the tensions in the community by reminding everyone that we were all on the same side – we all wanted marriage equality, whether we thought civil partnership was a good stepping stone or not. However, I reiterated that we did indeed want full marriage equality, and pointed out to the crowd that,

'Any asshole can get married. Any Fascist, any murderer, any sex offender can get married, but you cannot.'

The following Sunday a well-known columnist called Brenda Power took me to task in the *Sunday Times*, arguing against same-sex marriage. She trotted out the usual well-worn arguments, though the article reached a particularly silly nadir when she argued that *Panti is wrong on another point – homosexuals are entirely free to marry. They just can't marry someone of the same sex.* The tone of the article was condescending, and it lit a fire of anger in the community. The gay community is well used to people taking swipes at it, but it was the scornful, disrespectful tone of Power's piece that riled people. She dismissed me (as so many had before and would again) as a 'bloke in a dress', and the following week 'advised' the gay community that no one would take them seriously if they allowed their argument for equality to be articulated by a 'grown man' in 'fancy dress and a fright wig'. She disdainfully dismissed me as a man in a dress but would she have similarly dismissed a woman who spoke while wearing a suit? I imagine Brenda Power had no idea of the shit-storm she was about to bring down on herself, but the paper was soon flooded with angry emails – much to her shock – and the paper's editor was forced to defend the decision to print her piece. It became the subject of much heated debate online, in publications and on the airwaves, where it was the grist of phone-in talk shows and weekend discussions. Power and I were interviewed on various shows to defend our sides of the argument.

Occasionally commentators like Power find themselves the focus of real anger from the LGBT community and they are often confused as to why, but the 'why' is usually because of the tone of their remarks. If the gay community was to get angry with every commentator who argued against equality for gay people we'd have no time to do anything else. However, we are a community that is already sore and bruised from a lifetime of cuts delivered by schoolyard bullies, Christian preachers, conservative politicians, workplace managers, family, neighbours and Saturday-night drunks, so when a person in a position of power, like a newspaper columnist, uses their platform to sneer at us, we feel it deeply. We sit with our morning coffee over the paper, or at our work computer, and we are right back in the corner of the schoolyard with some hefty older boy holding our wrist and slapping us across the face with our own hand, laughingly demanding to know, 'Why are you hitting yourself?'

But Power had made another mistake. She wasn't to know it, but by singling Panti out she stoked greater anger, because the gay community was angry on my behalf. When she slagged off Panti she slagged off someone the gay community knew well. I've been ruining their nights out for years! To the younger ones I'm the slightly annoying drunk aunt who turns up at Christmas, and to the older ones I'm the queen who's been trotting out the same five numbers for the last twenty years. They may not all like me (!) but they all *know* me. I'm gay family. So, when Power singled me out for disdain she was slagging off family. The gays might think I'm an annoying, mouthy fool but I'm *their* annoying, mouthy fool. I'm their sister and they are allowed think it if they want, but Brenda Power is not.

So, a lot of the community took umbrage on my behalf. They circled their gay wagons around their mouthy cow, and fired off a volley of irate emails.

It was all a storm in a gay teacup, of course, but it was good to know that the gay community had my back, should I need it. And it reminded me once again that I had a voice – amplified by drag.

16. In the Eye of a Storm

I AM FORTY-FIVE YEARS old and I have never held hands unselfconsciously with a lover in public. That small everyday pleasure, so utterly taken for granted by most people, has never once been mine.

As with most gay people, there was a time in my young life when I struggled against being gay. I didn't want to be different. I didn't want to be this thing I didn't really understand, this thing I'd learned was shameful and joke-worthy. It took some time, but once I'd understood and accepted who and what I was, I have *never* wished it had turned out differently. I am entirely, deeply, thoroughly, relievedly happy to be gay. It suits me. Were I of a religious bent I would say I feel blessed to be gay.

Yet every day I'm jealous of straight people. I see them making those small, casual gestures of affection and intimacy carelessly in public and I'm jealous. I see a young couple strolling through the park, casually hand-in-hand, and I'm jealous. I see a teenage couple at a bus stop, she leaning into him, her hand in his, both tucked into his jacket pocket, and I'm jealous. I see a man unconsciously put a protective arm around his girlfriend's shoulders and she links her fingers in his without thinking and I'm jealous. I see an older woman stop and gesture to draw her husband's attention to something in a shop window; he takes her hand without thinking and they stand peering into the window discussing whatever drew her attention, hands unselfconsciously and casually joined, and I'm jealous.

Gay people don't get to hold hands in public without first considering the risk. We don't get to link arms or put a hand on a boyfriend's waist without first weighing up the possible consequences. We look around to see where we are, who's around. Is it late at night? What kind of area is it? Are there bored teenagers looking for amusement, lads outside pubs? Will we get sniggers? Taunts? Abuse? Worse? And if it seems safe enough we hold hands but those hands aren't casual and intimate, they are considered and weighed.

We walk along hand in hand trying hard to be carefree and normal, but we aren't. We're scanning the pavement ahead just in case, and when you see a group of blokes coming you determine to keep holding hands, defiantly, but now your small, intimate moment between two people in love has been turned into a political act of defiance, and it's ruined. And then you think what a lovely afternoon you've had and how all it will take is one spat 'Faggots!' or a cut lip to turn into a bad day so your hand slips out of his. Suddenly the distance between you seems gaping and filled with a kind of shame. And even if you're somewhere where you feel entirely safe, somewhere no one will react badly to your tiny gesture of affection – say, wandering through a posh department store – people will still notice. They may only notice, smile and think, *Isn't that nice to see two gays holding hands?* but they still *notice* and I don't want them to notice. I don't want our private moment turned into a *statement*. Like Schrödinger's cat, our small intimacy is altered simply be being observed.

Holding hands in public with a lover may seem like a small thing, but there are lots of small things – every day – that LGBT people have to put up with that others don't. Things we are expected to put up with, and count our blessings that we don't live in a country where we could be imprisoned or executed for being gay. Countless small adjustments we make, which others don't have to make, in order to be safe or not to be the object of scorn or ridicule. And we are so used to making those adjustments, so used to these small things, that we rarely even notice them ourselves any more. They are just part of the background of our lives, a constant malign presence that we have assimilated. We take these things for granted, as a given, simply part of *being*. If we complain, we are told we have nothing to complain about because aren't we lucky we don't live in Uganda or Russia?

But that's not good enough. It's not a game where the person who has it the worst wins the right to complain and everyone else has to shut up and put up. Our society is homophobic. It is infused with homophobia. Dripping with it and pervaded by it. And when you are forty-five years old and have spent thirty years putting up with it, thirty years absorbing those countless small slights and intimidations, sneers and occasionally much worse, you get tired of it. You get fed up putting up. You get fed up reading another article by another straight person telling you that you are somehow less than other people. You get fed up being described as 'intrinsically disordered' by people who don't know you from their celibate pulpits. You get fed up of scrawled graffiti and fed up of people sneeringly describing things as 'gay'. You get fed up of steeling yourself to walk past Saturday-night drunks hoping they won't notice you. And you get fed up with interfering busybodies using their time and energies to campaign against you being treated the same as every other citizen. People who organise meetings, make speeches, write letters to newspapers, appear on television and argue on radio all in an effort to have you separated out from everyone else and treated differently. Treated less. People whose bizarre obsession with the sexual life of other people won't let them simply let me live my life as I see fit. People who attempt at every turn to interfere in my life.

Of course I would prefer nobody to harbour any animosity towards or feel discomfort with gay people, but I can live with someone's personal and private casual homophobia. I don't mind if Mary in Wicklow sees Graham Norton on the telly and thinks, *He seems nice enough but does he have to be so gay?* I don't mind if Mary – who doesn't know any gay people apart from that fella who works in Curl Up & Dye and her only knowledge of gay people and their relationships is what she's picked up from schoolyards, *Coronation Street* and church – sees a report about same-sex marriage and thinks, *Oh, I'm not sure. I don't think that's a real marriage.* I can live with that. I'd hope that Mary would get to meet some gay people and find out that we are just the same, just as nice and just as annoying, as everyone else. I'd be happy to sit on the sofa and watch *Coronation Street* with her. And I'd be happy to have a cup of tea with her and talk to her about why she feels uncomfortable with the idea of gay relationships. And I'd hope she'd change her mind. For her own sake as much as anyone else's, because gay people are as capable of bringing goodness into her life as anyone else. And we could help her with the decorating.

But Mary's personal, private discomfort with 'the whole gay thing' is entirely different from the kind of homophobia that manifests itself in public.

A homophobia that manifests itself in an attempt to have LGBT people treated separately, differently, less. A homophobia that seeks to have LGBT people characterised as less worthy of respect. A homophobia that is enshrined in legislation and ensures that gay people are treated differently from their straight brothers and sisters. That kind of homophobia I *do* have a problem with, and LGBT people should be allowed to call it when they see it. It's our right to do so.

Religion, of course, has to shoulder much of the blame for our society's homophobia – most religions teach institutionalised homophobia and hold it up to be an admirable thing. Religion is certainly to blame for almost all of the people who actively campaign against equality for gay people because it gives their homophobia succour. It tells them they are good people as they whip up animus against gay people who are just trying to live their lives. It slaps them on the back as they rally for discrimination. They, of course, vehemently deny it. 'We don't hate you!' they cry. 'We love you! We love the sinner but hate the sin!' as if it's possible to separate the two. You can't separate the 'sinner' from the 'sin' when the so-called sin is an intrinsic and essential part of who you are. But no matter, because they will bend over backwards and tie themselves in ever more ridiculous moral and theological knots in an effort to excuse and justify their homophobia.

Many of the most vocal homophobes who argued against the decriminalisation of homosexual sex and every other advance for gay people since you'll now find amongst the ranks of those who argue against same-sex marriage, and it's quite the spectacle. They know they can't come right out and say what really drives them – an animus towards gay people and our relationships, and a disgust at what they imagine we do in bed – because they know people would roll their eyes and ignore them. So, around the world, the anti-same-sex-marriage crowd are forced to scramble for any other reason they can think of to argue their case. That gay people will destroy the institution of marriage (they won't, obviously); that gay people will adopt babies as accessories (sigh); that children raised by gay people are at a disadvantage (despite ample evidence to the contrary); that allowing gays to marry will destroy society (it hasn't and won't); that marriage has always meant one man and one woman (it hasn't); that marriage is solely designed for one purpose and one purpose only and that's children (it wasn't and isn't); and many more, including my own favourite, that the word 'marriage' is defined in some dictionary or other as meaning a union between a man and a woman and therefore same-sex marriages aren't marriages, which is a piffling argument against words and dictionaries and not an argument against same-sex marriage.

Apart from religion, the other real driver of homophobia is a disgust at gay sex, gay male sex in particular (lesbians just get caught in the homophobic crossfire, guilty by association): what they really don't like is anal sex. Buggery. Sodomy. And they imagine that that's all gay men do. They feverishly imagine that we spend all our time buggering each other. They obsess on it. In fact, they reduce us to this one sex act whether we do it or not.

We aren't people, with the same hopes, desires and feelings as everyone else: we are simply walking sex acts. Earlier this year I was invited to take part in the St Pat's For All parade in Queens, New York. It's a wonderful grassroots inclusive St Patrick's Day parade that was started in response to the ban on gay groups taking part in the famous Manhattan St Patrick's Day Parade. All kinds of Irish-American groups can take part in the Manhattan parade. Irish policemen can take part, Irish firemen, Irish community groups, Irish football players, Irish volleyball players, Irish dancers, Irish book clubs, Irish *anybody*. Except Irish gays.

The parade is organised by the Ancient Order of Hibernians, a kind of Catholic Orange Order, and I've seen one of its members on television defending the ban. He seemed like a nice ould fella, and he had a nice wife. They seemed happy together. And when I looked at them I saw a life lived together. I imagine that if I asked him about their life together he'd remember when they first met, how nervous he was on their first date. He'd remember the day he asked her to marry him, and how proud he was seeing her walk up the aisle in the dress she'd fretted over so much. I imagine he'd remember the day they moved into their first apartment and the day they finally bought their own small house. The time she went so far past her due date she threatened to bounce on a trampoline till the baby bounced out and they laughed hard. The time their youngest broke his leg and screamed crying all the way to the hospital, the time she got sick and he couldn't sleep in the empty bed and went back to the hospital even though he knew they wouldn't let him see her. He'd remember a life and a relationship full of all the things that make a person a person. And when I looked at them I imagined all those things too. But he doesn't look at me that way. He doesn't see gay people that way. As far as he and the organisers of that parade are concerned, gays are nothing more than sex acts, and sex acts have no place in their parade.[2]

On 11 January 2014, I appeared on RTÉ's *The Saturday Night Show*. The producers had approached me and we'd had a couple of meetings in the weeks before Christmas to talk about it. All of the discussion had focused on what kind of performance I would do – a stand-up bit, or a number, or something more theatrical. I suggested doing something similar to the kind of silly-but-fun stuff I do in my regular Pantibar show, where I re-edit scenes from movies and TV and recreate them as nutty lip-syncs. The producer and director were onboard immediately. There

---

[2] In 2014, after losing some of their major sponsors over the ban, the parade organisers agreed to let one LGBT group from within NBC, who broadcast the parade, march.

would be a sit-down interview with the host Brendan O'Connor after the performance, too, but everyone, including me, considered that the simple part. After all, it's a chat show, they interview people every week and I've been interviewed many times. What could go wrong?

A few days before the show aired I took the tram out to the studio of a sound engineer and we spent a few hours putting together a soundtrack for the performance, splicing together unrelated lines from various movies and TV shows and snippets from different songs to paint a picture of a woman becoming unhinged. The performance would begin with Panti in a dressing-room set, thinking to herself in voice-over when a phone would ring, interrupting her. She would answer it with a line from a movie, and another phone would ring, then another and another, faster and faster, Panti becoming more unhinged as each phone rang till eventually it reached a deranged crescendo. It was surreal and silly and fun.

As is usual, I did a 'pre-interview' on the phone with one of the researchers a few days before the show. It gives the researcher an idea of what kind of questions to prime the host to ask, and gives the interviewee an idea of the kind of questions that are likely to come up. And the kind of questions that were likely to come up were the usual things about how I got started in the drag business, what it's like being a drag queen, maybe a little about my background, where I'm from. There was some discussion about growing up gay in Ireland and what it's like for LGBT people now, but nothing that threw up any flags. All simple been-over-it-many-times-before stuff. Clearly I was intended to be a light segment in a light-entertainment show, and I can do that!

On the day of the show I went out to RTÉ with nothing more serious on my mind than what colour lipstick I'd wear. When I got there I chatted briefly with the researcher and the producer, then put my face on, got into costume and went down to studio to rehearse the performance. On the studio floor I bumped into the show's host, Brendan O'Connor, and we exchanged pleasantries before I and the crew rehearsed the performance, which was being shot on a small set in front of the live audience. There were a few adjustments to be made as we worked out camera angles and all the prop phones, but after a few run-throughs we were happy and I went back to my dressing room. At that point the researcher popped in and showed me Brendan's cue cards for the interview, which had on them all the questions he might ask me. There was nothing out of the ordinary so, after glancing through them, I amused myself by posting a silly 'selfie' on Twitter (What? All the kids are doing it) while waiting till the audience were in the studio and we were ready to shoot. The performance was being shot 'as live' about thirty minutes before the show went out to give me time to get out of makeup and costume because they wanted to do the interview with Rory rather than Panti. (People don't always appreciate that Panti is just a version of me. She's me refracted through another surface, and the lines between us are blurred. Her back-story is my back-story. The gay community understands that because they are so familiar with the kind of drag I do and have no difficulty speaking seriously with Panti.) The taped performance would be played, then Rory would come out to do the interview live.

The performance went smoothly and the primed studio audience responded enthusiastically. Then I took off my makeup, changed into a shirt and jacket, and went to the makeup room to get made up. I always do my own drag makeup because it's a specialised, special-effects job, and no one knows my face better than I do, but I'm happy to sit in the makeup chair for a light Rory TV face. Then I headed back to the studio and stood side stage with Brendan, chatting idly while we waited for the intro music. Then I waited a bit longer while he did his opening monologue and introduced Panti's performance. After that he introduced me and I walked into a shit-storm.

Not that I knew it immediately because at that point the shit-storm was only on the horizon and I didn't see it coming. The interview _seemed_ to go fine. Brendan asked me some questions, I answered them, we bantered a little, the audience laughed. Along the way Brendan asked me what it was like growing up gay and coming out when I did, and from there we wandered into a discussion about how attitudes to gay people have changed in Ireland since. It was in that context that I said that one of the only places where it's still okay to be 'horrible and mean' about gay people is in newspaper columns, at which point Brendan asked me which columnists I meant. In response to that direct question I mentioned *Irish Times* columnists Breda O'Brien and John Waters, then the Iona Institute (a Catholic lobby group whose members include Breda O'Brien) who regularly appear in print and on the airwaves to argue against same-sex marriage.

Brendan said he wouldn't have considered John Waters to be homophobic – a word I hadn't actually used – and in response I ... well, it's probably best if you see for yourself exactly what I said:

Rory O'Neill: '... but of course I've met people who have just absolutely had awful, terrible experiences coming out to their families and ...'

Brendan O'Connor: 'But a lot has changed, hasn't it, since then, like?'

RO'N: 'So much has changed. And I think, em, a small country like Ireland, sometimes we get a bad rap because people think, Oh, small conservative country blah blah blah. But actually I think a small country like Ireland changes much faster than a big country because absolutely ... I'm ... Think about it. Every single person in this audience has

a cousin or a neighbour or the guy that you work
with who is a flaming queen. I mean you all know
one. And it's very hard to hold prejudices against
people when you actually know those people.
And Ireland, because it's such small communities
grouped together, everybody knows the local gay
and, you know, maybe twenty years ago it was
OK to be really mean about him but nowadays it's
just not OK to be really mean about him. The only
place that you see it's OK to be really horrible and
mean about gays is, you know, on the internet in
the comments and, you know, people who make a
living writing opinion pieces for newspapers. You
know there's a couple of them that really cheese—'

At that point, Brendan asked:

BO'C: 'Who are they?'

And I said:

RO'N: 'Oh, well, the obvious ones. You know, Breda
O'Brien [*Irish Times* columnist] today – oh, my
God, you know banging on about gay priests and
all. The usual suspects, the John Waters [then *Irish
Times* columnist] and all of those people, the Iona
Institute crowd. I mean I just, you know, just … Feck
off! Get the hell out of my life. Get out of my life. I
mean [applause from audience], why … it astounds
me … astounds me that there are people out there
in the world who devote quite a large amount of

their time and energies to trying to stop people, you
know, achieving happiness because that is what the
people like the Iona Institute are at.'

I'm afraid I lied to you. You can't see for yourself exactly
what I said because the lawyers won't let me show
you any more. Not because, as people have been led to
believe, I named anyone as homophobes (I didn't) but
because what was said next would become the subject of
an almighty furore and legal action.

But I can *tell* you what happened next.

Brendan introduced the term 'homophobic', saying
he would not consider John Waters to be homophobic.
It wasn't a word I had used or even given particular
thought to, and I felt uncomfortable when he brought it
up. I hadn't gone on the show to talk about any particular
individuals, or label anyone homophobic, so in response
I chose to talk in general terms about homophobia, and
gave a nuanced description of what I believe the term to
mean – not in relation to any individual or group, but in
a general sense. I am aware that the word 'homophobia'
can be provocative and it needs to be given context,
which is what I sought to do – and to keep the tone
neutral and general, not personal.

Homophobia, I said, like any form of discrimination,
can be a subtle thing. I said I didn't believe that
homophobes are all horrible monsters who go around
beating up gay people, and I suggested that we *all* have
a tendency towards homophobia and the best thing we
can do is to be aware of it and work on being better.

My position has always been that if you argue that gay people should be treated differently to everybody else, or that their relationship should be considered in any way less than everybody else's relationship, then although you may be a good person, and although some of your best friends may be gay, I'm sorry but yes, you do have a problem with homophobia. And that, in a nutshell, is what I said – my honestly held opinion.

It had gone out live, and before I had even left the studio Shirley Temple Bar had taken the 'selfie' I had posted online from the dressing room and reposted it, overlaid with a quote from the interview, 'FECK OFF OUTTA MY LIFE!' but, still, for the most part the interview was light and uncontentious and, as far as I was concerned, it had all gone well. And it was clear that those involved in the show thought so, too, because after the segment they were very happy and there were thanks and air-kisses and hugs goodbye. And if, over the next few days, you had asked me how it had gone, I would have said casually, 'What? The TV thing? Yeah, it was fine.'

The first inkling I got that something was up was a day or two later when my sister, who hadn't seen the show when it was broadcast, called and said she had tried to find it online but it seemed to be gone from the RTÉ website. I assumed it was just a technical glitch and I didn't give it much thought. Then, on maybe the Tuesday, I got a call from someone at the show to check my bank details (I was paid the standard appearance fee that all performers get) and in passing I mentioned to her that the show wasn't online any more, and she mentioned that it had been taken down on foot of a letter from John Waters. I was taken aback, but even then I assumed it was a simple matter and something entirely between Waters and RTÉ.

Then, a couple of days later, I got two solicitors' letters via e-mail, and the next day two more. A few days after that I discovered I had received a fifth, which had been sent via regular mail and had sat unnoticed in Pantibar till I went to collect the hard copies of the letters. The letters were all written by the same solicitor, but on behalf of five different clients who were each claiming that I had defamed them. Two of the letters were on behalf of Breda O'Brien and John Waters, and the other three were on behalf of individual members of the Iona Institute whom I hadn't mentioned at all, including its founder and director, the columnist and commentator David Quinn. One of those three people I'd never even heard of before and another I was only vaguely aware of. All five letters were almost identical and the assertion was that I had made 'seriously defamatory comments', which implied that their client 'is known and disliked by the gay community as a person who promotes homophobia and hatred for homosexuals and the gay community generally'. They were demanding that I immediately provide them with an 'open written apology' and retraction confirming that I 'accept that there were no grounds whatsoever' for my comments, and that I accept that 'many people who saw [my] interview would think less of [their] client and in particular, the gay and lesbian community would think less of [their] client'.

Getting the letters was a shock. I had made the comments off the cuff and I had only named O'Brien, Waters and the Iona Institute in response to a direct question from Brendan O'Connor, the host of a chat show on the national broadcaster. And even then I had only accused them of being 'horrible and mean about gays', which is merely my honestly held opinion. I considered my comments to have been reasonable and nuanced.

At the time I knew very little about our arcane defamation laws so, sitting on my sofa with the dog, reading the first letters, I assumed they were silly and vexatious. Nonetheless, these were letters on behalf of prominent people, probably wealthier and much more legally and politically savvy than I, so I wasn't going to ignore them. I called a barrister friend and explained the situation, and he recommended a good solicitor he knew called Andrew Sheridan, who knew his way around a defamation case. Thankfully, my new best friend Andrew agreed to help me.

Andrew is a neatly put together guy with a lawyerly demeanour. Controlled and serious but with flashes of humour or steely determination – and the occasional bit of Law Library gossip – he speaks deliberately, meaning what he says and saying what he means. It was clear from the beginning that he thought this was an interesting case and I could tell he quite relished the idea of taking on my correspondents. However, like all lawyers, he can be infuriating because, knowing the vagaries of the law and the unpredictability of courtrooms and juries, he'll never give you a straight yes-or-no answer. He'll tell you what he thinks is the likely outcome, what he educatedly guesses to be the probable outcome, but always leaves room for doubt – always allows room for the possibility that it will all go tits up in court. As he started to explain the seriousness of the situation I was in, and the incomprehensible complexities of our defamation laws, I started to want a straight answer. I wanted to say, 'Yeah, but it'll all be fine in the end, right?' and I wanted him to say, 'Yes', but he couldn't.

What he could and did mention was bankruptcy – *my* bankruptcy – which was a distinct possibility, apparently. Still, after enquiring into the state of my finances, he told me that the only people who could afford to take on a defamation case were the very rich, and the very poor because they have nothing to lose, 'and you have nothing to lose'.

What Andrew wanted to know was what I wanted to do. Was I prepared to go to court over this, a process that could take years of stress with no guarantee of the outcome? Was I prepared to possibly lose what little I had over it? If we lost in the High Court we could conceivably go all the way to the European courts, but was I prepared even to contemplate that? Six or seven years of stress with this hanging over me?

The truth was, I didn't know. I needed more time to think. I was being asked to apologise, but I didn't have anything to apologise for. I'd meant what I said. I believed what I'd said. And people can say lots of things about me but what they can't say is that I'm not principled because I am my parents' child and I got that from them. I have risked things and lost things before on a point of principle, and I was prepared to do it again. I would avoid court if I could, but I wouldn't apologise for something I hadn't done. That was my line in the sand. 'OK,' Andrew said. 'Then we'll work from there.'

I was beginning to understand that I could really be in trouble but Andrew seemed to know what he was doing and I felt I was in good hands. Like the sick and injured animals that cleaved to my father and refused to leave after he'd treated them, I fell a little bit in love with Andrew too.

The next two weeks were difficult. Stressful, worrying, upsetting and tiring. I didn't sleep well and would wake up suddenly to find my dog Penny sitting up on the bed looking at me oddly. And I was angry. Why were these people so upset? I mean, if you're going to write, or publicly advocate for gay people to be treated differently from everyone else, then own it. Don't advocate for gay people to be treated differently from everyone else and then get your knickers in a twist when somebody suggests that that might be construed as homophobic. And since when did 'homophobe' become the worst thing you could call someone? So terrible that even people who publicly advocate for gay people to be treated differently from everyone else are appalled at the suggestion. And, anyway, the easy way to stop people thinking you might be a homophobe is to stop publicly advocating for gay people to be treated differently from everyone else!

I spent a lot of time discussing the case with Andrew and how we would respond to the letters. He made contact with RTÉ's legal department and was told that RTÉ had received similar solicitors' letters from the same five people, and a sixth from another member of the Iona Institute. At that point RTÉ's legal team said they were considering their own response but assured Andrew they would keep him in the loop regarding how they intended to proceed. We were very eager that this would be the case, given that RTÉ's decisions could have serious consequences for my own position. However, it soon became clear that we would not be kept in the loop. Emails went unanswered, meetings failed to materialise and we had little contact after that. What little we did have didn't inspire confidence. RTÉ were in disarray, floundering around in a panic, desperately trying to make this all go away. It was difficult not to form the opinion that we were an annoyance they also wanted to go away.

I did have a few telephone conversations with a couple of the people who work on *The Saturday Night*

Show and they told me what they knew but they were clearly confused as to what was going on as things had been taken over their heads to RTÉ's top brass.

During this time it was not a mainstream media story. Painfully aware of the shortcomings of our defamation laws, most newspapers and broadcasters were terrified to touch it. The removal of my interview from the internet was noted in the most bland terms, and a couple of small, timid pieces reported that the show was the subject of legal action, but little more than that made it into print. Not that it stopped reporters trying, and my phone was now ringing off the hook. One paper tried four times over those first two weeks to get a substantial article past their own lawyers but to no avail. And when a student newspaper, the *Trinity News*, broke ranks and published a lengthy opinion piece that supported me, they, too, received a solicitor's letter from Waters.

Online, things were different and it immediately became a big story there, spread by blogs and social media. Debate raged on Facebook, Twitter and forums. To some this was a clear case of homophobia and censorship; RTÉ were craven for taking my interview down, and the Iona Institute were bullies, using threats of legal action to silence their critics. To others, I was a jumped-up drag queen defaming decent people with ludicrous accusations on national TV; not only should RTÉ have taken down the interview, they should be ashamed of ever having given me airtime. Of course, this being the internet, people also said many worse things about all of us.

As the debate raged online, RTÉ quietly put the interview back on their website but with the 'offending' portion edited out, and in a statement to a reporter they said it had been removed due to 'potential legal issues'.

Meanwhile Andrew advised that if I was not going to withdraw my remarks then the best course of action was to respond forcefully and at length to each of the complainants. We would tell them in no uncertain terms that I had nothing to apologise for, then set out our general arguments refuting their claims. To do this properly, we would need to research exactly what each of the complainants and the Iona Institute had ever written or said on the subject of LGBT people or same-sex marriage. This would be a big task (already made easier by internet sleuths who were delighting in digging up old interviews and opinion pieces), so Andrew suggested I speak to one of the marriage-equality groups and anyone else I knew who might have a head start in this area and see if they might help.

I had at this stage already been inundated with offers of help from various people – including a lot of lawyers! – so it was easy to get a group together. One evening about ten people – journalists, activists, academics and organisers – gathered in the basement of Pantibar to see what they already had that might help and what more they could do. While everyone there was committed to helping me fight my case and hopefully avoid court, it was also clear that the LGBT activists in the group were also excited at the prospect of the fight against their erstwhile opponents (especially the Iona Institute, which has long campaigned against marriage equality and had only recently made an extremely controversial presentation against it to the Constitutional Convention). It was a fight they were sure they would win in the court of public opinion even if I lost in the court of law.

A fight like this, especially with Panti at its sharp end, would also energise the LGBT community in the campaign for same-sex marriage. So, for the LGBT activists there, this situation was a win. I, on the other hand, wasn't so sure. I could envisage a time in the not very far future when I would be broke, trudging penniless and bankrupt through the courts, while the rest of the gays were celebrating their gay marriages and dropping the kids off at school.

Then, two weeks after the original broadcast, without any consultation with Andrew, Brendan O'Connor uncomfortably read out an apology on behalf of RTÉ.

On *The Saturday Night Show* two weeks ago comments were made by a guest, suggesting the journalist and broadcaster John Waters, Breda O'Brien and some members of the Iona institute are homophobic. These are not the views of RTÉ and we would like to apologise for any upset or distress caused to the individuals named or identified. It is an important part of democratic

debate that people must be able to hold dissenting
views on controversial issues.

Andrew was furious. In one of the only conversations
he'd had with RTÉ's legal team they had assured him that
they were not considering an apology and that, in any
case, they wouldn't be making any decisions 'for weeks
and weeks'. He was also furious because the wording of
the apology was a brazen attempt to shift any possible
blame to me, when all I had done was answer a direct
question from the show's presenter. Not forgetting,
too, that it hadn't been 'a guest' who had introduced
the word that had got everyone so hot under the collar,
but their man! Of course, the whole thing had lawyerly
fingerprints all over it, especially the last line, which
attempted to have its cake and eat it by not identifying
whose 'views' were 'dissenting' or 'controversial'. Theirs
or mine? Clearly the implication was that I was the one
denying people 'the right to hold dissenting views' and
impeding 'democratic debate'.

I was fucking furious. What they were attempting to
do was throw me under the bus. RTÉ were essentially
standing up in the classroom and pointing at me
shouting, 'He did it, sir! He did it!' Evidently, as far as
RTÉ were concerned, it was every man for himself.

I was furious, too, at the lily-liveredness of it. It was
craven. Supine. And it was a derogation of their duty
as a public broadcaster. RTÉ is not Coca-Cola. They are

not a private company with only one responsibility: to do what's best for the company. They are a national broadcaster, publicly funded, with a remit to provide a platform for free and open debate, to facilitate the 'democratic debate' their mealy mouthed apology pretended was so important to them. And yet all it took for Iona to bring them to heel was a few quid to a solicitor for a handful of letters. RTÉ should have had some balls and (in the equivalent legal terminology) told them to go fuck themselves, but instead they caved. And for good measure offered me up instead.

And just why were Iona and Waters so quick to run to their solicitor? O'Brien, Quinn and Waters are all opinion columnists, with regular columns in national newspapers (and all appear regularly on radio and TV) to espouse their opinions on any subject they please, including – as they all have – on gay people and our relationships. They are well used to the cut and thrust of vigorous debate, and all of them could simply have denounced me from their platforms in the country's most-read national newspapers, so why did they go running to their lawyers? No gay person is in any doubt as to these people's opinions on our relationships because they assaults us from the pages of our newspapers and ruin our lazy Sunday-morning breakfasts.

John Waters has since taken issue with the suggestion that he 'campaigns' against same-sex marriage and that may be true in the sense that, unlike the Iona

Institute, it's not one of his main bugbears, but he has used his platform to espouse his views on gay people, their relationships and their motives. And he pulls no punches. For instance, in an interview in the UCD *College Tribune* in August 2012, he claimed that gay marriages are a 'satire' on marriage, that gay people don't actually 'want to get married; they want to destroy the institution of marriage because they're envious of it', and that our real motive is 'a deliberate sabotage of the culture and the relishing of the destruction as a result'.

He has also said in that interview (and later defended his remarks in another interview) during a discussion about adoption:

Well, you know, if two brothers applied to adopt a child, they'd be laughed out of court but the fact that they're buggering each other would make a difference, would it?

Leaving aside the bizarre leap to incest, it is, of course, a facetious and pointless argument as the same question could be asked about a brother and sister but, more importantly, it is a perfect example of an attempt to reduce gay people to a sex act. Gay couples aren't in loving relationships, like everybody else, they are merely buggering each other. And the choice of the word 'buggering' is deliberate, too, as it's a blunter, cruder term more likely to offend than the usual 'having sex'.

So, the question remains: why did these journalists and commentators threaten to sue? Why, with all the platforms at their disposal to refute my remarks, did they come after RTÉ and me with legal threats? And do it while at the same time claiming that I was the one trying to stifle open debate by using the word 'homophobia'.

Of course I can't know why they did it, but I can hazard a guess. I think they did it partly because they thought I'd be a soft target. They dismissed me as a bloke in a dress who doesn't really have a voice. And perhaps thought, correctly, that RTÉ would be a soft target, too. RTÉ had only just been through the Father Kevin Reynolds case where the station's flagship current affairs programme had falsely accused the priest of fathering a child through rape. When it was eventually proved that the allegations were entirely false, after Reynolds's reputation had been destroyed, it was forced to apologise and pay substantial damages. It was a low point for the broadcaster, and in the aftermath it was skittish and easily frightened by a solicitor's letter claiming defamation.

Clearly RTÉ was the real target. Oh, I suspect they didn't like me – I imagine they still don't! – but RTÉ was the big fish they wanted to fry. Iona was well aware that the country would no doubt soon be heading to the polls to vote on same-sex marriage and I believe they decided they couldn't let RTÉ, the national broadcaster with the power to have a huge impact on the result of a poll, allow the word 'homophobia' to be introduced to the debate because, they figured, if that happened, the game was up for them. They couldn't allow people to suggest that their arguments against marriage equality were simply based on a dislike of gay people.

I was so furious about RTÉ's apology that Andrew sent them a letter threatening to sue them, claiming that their apology had in fact defamed me with its implication that RTÉ had no real role in the débâcle, and that I had 'gone rogue' on the show, with RTÉ only an unfortunate, innocent broadcaster. Their apology, we said, was injurious to my reputation: it suggested that I couldn't be trusted and posed an enhanced risk as a media guest. I had decided not to actually follow up with my threat, but I thought the spineless eejits could do with a shot across the bow. But the substance of my complaint was true. I meant it, and it was soon to be borne out: for a long time afterwards, whenever I was interviewed on radio or TV, nervous producers would insist on a pre-record – until eventually I put a foot down and refused to do pre-records on principle. Even now, I always get an embarrassed producer or researcher mumbling that 'Eh, you know ... just ... If you could just make sure not to mention any names.'

The moment the apology was broadcast, things started to move up a gear. People were outraged. The online debate escalated, with RTÉ being denounced as having given in to censorship and bullying. And the apology pushed the whole affair onto the pages and into the airwaves of the mainstream media. They couldn't continue to ignore the story when an apology had been broadcast.

Then I got a phone call from someone in RTÉ. They told me that the staff was in an uproar about it. There had been meetings in which the management had attempted to explain their position to an unreceptive audience, and memos had been sent to all staff. The most interesting thing they told me was that the gossip in RTÉ was that the six complainants had also received a substantial payout: rumour ran that it was close to a hundred thousand euro.

I was shocked. Surely that couldn't be true. Could RTÉ really have been that easy a pushover? And almost a hundred thousand euro? It *couldn't* be true! I wouldn't have been at all surprised if I'd heard that RTÉ had paid out a small nominal sum – a hundred euro in the 'poor box' as a token – but *that* sum? Could people like Quinn, O'Brien and Waters really be that tone deaf to public opinion? These people were media professionals. Hell, the Iona Institute's *raison d'être* was to influence and manage public opinion. Could they really have so misread the public mood? Because I was certain if this turned out to be true, and if it became widely known, then lots of people who had previously been apathetic about the whole affair would be pushed firmly into my camp.

Any money RTÉ paid out was licence payers' money. And a payout would make the complainants look money-grubbing and greedy. They'd already got their apology so why go after the money? But the person on the phone insisted the gossip must be true. RTÉ was a small town and everybody knew everybody else's business.

I knew that if it turned out to be true it would be a big help to me. I had already realised that I had very little in my armoury to fight this, and the one hope I *had* had – that RTÉ would be on my side – was already long gone. My only weapon was noise. I needed to make as much noise as possible. I needed to kick up a storm and get as many people as possible on my side – because otherwise I was fucked. I knew that if it became public knowledge that RTÉ had made a substantial payout to powerful people – people who had other options than legal ones – then that would make a lot of noise.

I couldn't verify if it was true or not but I didn't need to. Someone else could do that. I sent a text to a couple of journalists I was friendly with, saying what I'd heard, knowing damn well they'd be sniffing round RTÉ before I'd even hung up. And for good measure I sent out a vague tweet saying that I would be shocked if the rumour regarding a payout was true. I knew that would be enough.

The next day it was front-page news (€85,000 was the generally accepted figure) and the Iona confirmed it with a statement on their website. All hell broke loose.

The internet exploded with indignation. The story led the news bulletins. RTÉ and the Broadcasting Authority were flooded with complaints. Questions were raised in the Dáil. It was discussed and debated and dissected on radio and television, and I was fielding calls from what felt like every reporter in the country. They were still having some trouble getting much beyond the bare facts past their legal departments but they were trying. And, of course, the other radio and TV channels were delighted to kick RTÉ when it was down. And I was happy to talk to them and appear on their shows because all this noise, this cacophony of outrage, would, I hoped, enable me to get across my side of the story.

The whole sorry saga had touched a nerve. It chimed with a public mood and a particular point in the country's evolution on LGBT rights. People saw it as an affront to the LGBT community generally. We weren't being allowed to call, as they saw it, a spade a spade. We were being put in our gay place. But, more than that, ordinary people saw a group of powerful people – establishment people, people with access to national platforms – telling everyone else to shut up and pocketing their money while they were at it. Although it seemed to come as a shock to them, these people weren't universally liked, but most ordinary people had been previously too polite to say so. The people who took the money didn't realise quite how far out of step they were with most regular folk. Most Irish people have a gay brother or a lesbian daughter or best friend, and they took umbrage on their behalf.

Two thousand people turned up to a hastily organised protest in Dublin city centre on a grey Sunday afternoon to denounce 'homophobia and RTÉ censorship'. I stood at the back, somewhat embarrassed and astounded that so many people cared.

The other consequence of the apology and the payout was that it probably meant it was less likely that I'd end up in court. After all, they'd fried their big fish: what benefit would it be to them to come after me? I had nothing to give them. I had a bar that had managed to scrape through the recession but it had Panti's name above the door and would be worthless without it. Not ending up in court would suit me just fine so Andrew and I decided to change our planned response to the initial letters. Instead of responding forcefully and vigorously, we would respond with a *slightly* more conciliatory tone. I wouldn't apologise (that was still my line in the sand) but there was no need to poke a wounded tiger. Andrew sent a letter asking their solicitor if his clients 'believe they have achieved satisfaction in this matter'. We received no reply.

I had appeared on *The Saturday Night Show* on 11 January, and two weeks later, on the twenty-fifth, Brendan O'Connor read out the apology that would explode the story out of the internet and onto the front pages. In the middle of that week, while I was trying to keep my head above water in the boiling cauldron of public opinion, the Abbey Theatre invited me to speak.

17. The Noble Call

FIACH MAC CONGHAIL IS THE energetic, astute, glad-handing, mischievous director of Ireland's national theatre. He's a doer, the kind of man who could have been a Celtic Tiger property developer cutting a swathe through Dublin with glass and steel if he'd wanted, but he was interested in developing the arts, not offices. He's not afraid to ruffle a few feathers, either. He has a touch of the P. T. Barnum about him, and he delights in the Abbey's history of provocation. No doubt, had he been director in 1907 when people rioted in protest at the theatre's production of *The Playboy of the Western World*, Fiach would have stood at his office window and congratulated himself on a job well done. I suspect he regards ruffling the occasional feather as part of a national theatre's job.

When he first invited me to address the audience at the end of the final performance of the theatre's production

of James Plunkett's *The Risen People*, my first instinct was
to say, 'No.' I was in the eye of a media storm while at
the same time trying to get on with my regular work. My
hands were already full and I was tired. I didn't have the
time or the energy to start thinking about making some
kind of speech at the national bloody theatre! But I did
give it some thought, and I changed my mind. And while
it would probably be a little over-dramatic to say that that
decision changed my life, it is certainly true that it had a
greater impact on it than I could ever have imagined.

It was definitely one of the best decisions I ever made.

I agreed to do it partly because I know the people at
the Abbey and they've always been good to me. I had
done various things there over the previous few years
and, only a few months before, my show *All Dolled Up*
had run there for a week on the Peacock stage. However,
the real reason I agreed to do it was that, up until that
point, I had been talked *about* a lot, and guardedly
talked *to* with nervous lawyers and producers hovering
over my shoulder. The Abbey would be different. This
would be my first opportunity to give my side of the
story, directly, without the filter of skittish lawyers or
heavy-handed producers. Of course, I imagined that
the only people who would ever hear what I had to say
were the people in the auditorium that night, but that
was enough: I was doing it for *me*. In the midst of all the
madness, this was a welcome opportunity to speak my
mind, and Fiach assured me I could say what I wanted.

The Risen People is a drama set among the grinding poverty of Dublin's tenements in 1913, during the general strike known as the Lockout. The production had been running for the previous two months and, at the end of every performance, a different person had 'answered the noble call'. The Noble Call is an Irish pub tradition, like a party piece, where everyone must sing a song or recite a poem, and the Abbey had invited a long list of artists, musicians, writers, thinkers, polemicists and more to take to the stage and respond in any way they wanted to the production. Mine would be the very last Noble Call, after the cast's final performance. Two nights before, I went along to see the production with my friend and collaborator Phillip. I knew that I wanted to speak about the 'Pantigate' affair but I wasn't sure until I saw the production how that might relate to the play.

That night it was the turn of socialist politician and activist Richard Boyd Barrett to answer the Noble Call. Richard is a smart guy and, no stranger to public speaking, he spoke engagingly and recited a long, difficult poem from memory. However, the audience had just sat through a two-hour play and so were perhaps a little too tired to engage fully with his fairly intellectual choice. His address was livened up somewhat when he was heckled by an expensively dressed posh-voiced woman, who was in no mood to listen to a socialist on her night out at the theatre and grumbled loudly throughout, much to the rest of the audience's amused disapproval.

Watching Richard, I decided I would be better off doing something more personal.

The next day I let it percolate in the back of my mind and thought vaguely about what I might want to say as I tried to keep up with the continuing media storm. That night when I went to bed, I lay there and started to put some order on my thoughts. At one point, I sat up and tapped a few notes into my phone.

The next day was Saturday, always a busy day for me. My dog Penny needs to be walked first, and then I have to prepare for my regular Saturday-night show in Pantibar: make a running order, talk to the guest performers about what they're doing, pick the tracks and scenes I'll be doing, put the show's tracks onto my computer, maybe learn some lines or go to Boots to pick up nails or hairspray. So, I didn't have a lot of time, but in the afternoon I sat down for a couple of hours and wrote a speech. I didn't labour over it because I knew essentially what I wanted to say. I was really just getting some things off my chest, and was hoping to remind people what this whole kerfuffle was really about: I was frustrated that the media were becoming bogged down in a kind of school-debating-team-style discussion over the dictionary definition of the word 'homophobia'. I didn't write out the whole speech, word for word. I wrote a solid framework but left myself room just to speak, rather than remember. It's how I work best. As long as I hit the key points and the rhetorically important sentences, the rest would look after itself. I ran through it once or twice in my living room in front of Penny (she seemed unimpressed), then went to Pantibar to get ready in my dressing room there.

It had been arranged to film my Noble Call for YouTube, but as I put on my face in the mirror, I still thought that the only people who would ever hear it were the five hundred or so people in the auditorium that night, and perhaps a few hundred more might stumble across it later online. A few days earlier I had mentioned I was going to be giving a speech in the Abbey to filmmaker and photographer Conor Horgan. I have known Conor since he first photographed me for the Alternative Miss Ireland poster in 1996, and he did so for nearly every one over the next eighteen years. I like and trust Conor, so when he approached me a few years ago and asked if he could make a documentary around me, I agreed reluctantly. Despite what people might imagine, I'm actually quite a reserved person. Panti is the outgoing one. I'm also my mother's child and she abhors anyone making a show of or getting 'notions' about themselves. The idea of someone following me, Rory, around with a camera fills me with dread.

However, it's hard to say no to Conor so for the last few years he's been turning up every now and then with a camera and a microphone. From the beginning I decided to take an entirely hands-off approach to his documentary – this was his project, nothing to do with me, really – but whenever I'm doing anything that I think might be of interest to him, I let him know. When I mentioned the Abbey speech he was eager to shoot it. Conor, of course, had been absolutely thrilled when I stumbled into a media storm: before that I don't think he was entirely sure what his documentary was really about, but now all his gay ships had come in on a tide of scandal. I think the filmmaker in him was probably secretly hoping I'd die in a very dramatic accident or something, and now, in a way, I had! He arranged to shoot my Noble Call with another friend, Caroline Campbell, a whip-smart lawyer and activist, who also makes short films and who'd been eagerly following the Pantigate drama.

Also very enthusiastic to have the speech filmed was Brian Barrington, the friend who'd recommended and introduced me to my solicitor, Andrew. Brian had kept in close touch with Andrew and me throughout, giving advice, making suggestions and dissecting each day's developments. Brian is very savvy when it comes to the media and an enthusiastic devourer of blogs and online publications, so he was especially eager to get the speech filmed and posted online. He didn't know what I was going to say, but he trusted I wouldn't do a horrible job.

The night before the speech, he wondered in an email to me if giving the speech in drag was the best idea. He worried it might frighten the horses. It might be offputting to regular folk not used to seeing drag queens every day. It might be confrontational – perhaps come between me and my message.

I was determined to do it in drag.

Partly because I had no choice – I was going to have to jump straight into a cab afterwards and rush back to Pantibar to my show. And partly because I knew I would be much more comfortable giving the speech as Panti. Standing on stages and talking to people is what Panti *does*. It's what she's good at, what she's been doing for twenty-five years. Rory, on the other hand, would be much less comfortable.

But the real reason I was sure I should do it in drag was because I knew the drag would help me. I'd learned many years ago at that disastrous Christmas gig in Galway that a drag queen grabs people's attention in a way that a guy in a shirt and trousers can't ever hope to compete with. And I knew that, rather than get in the way of my message, drag would *amplify my voice*. It would help to get me heard above the cacophony. I knew what Brian meant, though: most of the audience in the theatre (or watching on computers at home) would probably not be familiar with drag queens, and when I first walked out they would be blinded by the drag. At first they wouldn't be able to see past it, wouldn't be able to *hear* past it. And they would come with a lot of preconceived notions about drag queens, what they do and what they are capable of. They would expect me to be brash and outrageous and silly. They would expect me to be light. But I was aware of that and knew how to handle it. I would start off with a light preamble, let them get to know me a little, let them get used to the tone of my voice, my accent, my cadence, let them look all they needed to till they had answered their own questions about my hair, my makeup, my corset, my breasts. I'd give them a moment to get past that and settle. I'd give them a minute to relax, draw them in, and when they were ready, I'd tell them what I'd come to say.

When I was ready Phillip and another good friend called Ian came to pick me up, and we took a cab to the theatre. On the way, Phillip, who knows me well and has worked with me many times, archly asked, 'So, did you write something?' knowing full well it was possible I'd been lazy and decided to wing it.

'Yes, Phillip,' I replied, matching his archness. 'I did write something. I think it's pretty good too.' Then, jokingly, I remarked that if I could wring a tear out of one of those emotional actress types I'd be happy.

Ian looked suddenly concerned. 'You're not going to do something *serious*, are you?' He was clearly convinced that I was about to embarrass them all in front of five hundred people, on the stage of the national bloody theatre.

When we arrived, about fifteen minutes before the night's performance was scheduled to end, Conor was there with his camera and someone from the Abbey greeted us. I left Phillip and Ian waiting in the lobby for the performance to finish so they could slip into the auditorium, and I walked around the theatre to the stage door and went backstage where I waited in the wings till the cast had done their bows.

One of the actors introduced me. In a nice coincidence it was an actor I knew, a lovely guy, who had once borrowed a wig and shoes off me for a role he was playing. I never got them back.

'Tonight,' he said, 'we are delighted to welcome to the stage Ireland's most fabulous drag queen and famous activist, Panti.'

I walked out of the dark, the click of my heels sounding above the applause for this creature who had magically walked straight off the day's front pages and onto the stage.

Hello. My name is Panti, and for the benefit of the visually impaired or the incredibly naïve, I am a drag queen. I am also a performer of sorts, and an accidental and occasional gay rights activist.

As you may have already gathered, I am also painfully middle class. My father was a country vet, I went to a nice school, and afterwards to that most middle class of institutions – an art college. And, although this may surprise some of you, I have always found gainful employment in my chosen field – gender discombobulation.

So the kind of grinding, abject poverty that we saw so powerfully on stage tonight is something that I can thankfully say I have no experience of.

But I do know a little something about oppression. Or, at least, oppression is something that I can relate to. Now, I am not, of course, for a minute going to compare my situation to that of Dublin workers in 1913, but I do know what it feels like to be put in your place.

Have any of you ever been standing at a pedestrian crossing when a car goes by and in it are a bunch of lads, and they lean out the window as they go by and shout, 'Fag!' and throw a carton of milk at you? Oh, it doesn't really hurt. I mean, after all, it's just a wet carton and, in many ways, they're right – I am a fag. So it doesn't hurt, but it feels oppressive.

And when it really does hurt is afterwards. Because it's afterwards that I wonder and worry and obsess – what was it about me? What did they see in me? What was it that gave me away? And I hate myself for wondering that. It feels oppressive, and the next time that I'm standing at a pedestrian crossing, I hate myself for it but I check myself to see what is it about me that gives the gay away. And I check myself to make sure that I'm not doing it this time.

Have you ever come home in the evening and turned on the television and there is a panel of people – nice people, respectable people, smart people, the kind of people who probably make good neighbourly neighbours, the kind of people who write for newspapers – and they are all sitting around, and they are having a reasoned debate on the television. A reasoned debate about you. About what kind of a person you are, about whether or not you are capable of being a good parent, about whether you want to destroy marriage, about whether or not you are safe around children, about whether or not God herself thinks you are an abomination, about whether in fact you are 'intrinsically disordered'. And even the nice TV presenter lady that you feel is like almost a friend because you see her being nice on TV all the time, even she thinks it's perfectly OK that they are all having this reasoned debate about you, and about who you are, and what rights you 'deserve' or don't deserve. And that feels oppressive.

Have you ever been on a crowded train with one of your best gay friends, and inside a tiny part of you is cringing because he is being so gay, and you find yourself trying to compensate for his gayness by butching up a little, or by trying to steer the conversation onto safer, 'straighter', territory? Now this is you, who have spent the last thirty-five years of your life trying to be the best gay possible, and yet there is still this small part of you that is embarrassed by his gayness.

And I hate myself for that, and that feels

oppressive. And when I am standing at a pedestrian bloody light I am checking myself.

Have you ever gone into your favourite neighbourhood café with the paper that you buy every day, and you open it up and inside is a five-hundred-word opinion, written by a nice, middle-class woman? The kind of woman who probably gives to charity, the kind of woman whom you would be totally happy to leave your children with. And she is arguing over five hundred words – so reasonably – about whether or not you should be treated less than everybody else. Arguing that you should be given fewer rights than everybody else. And when you read that, and then the woman at the next table gets up and excuses herself to squeeze by you and smiles at you and you smile back and nod and say, 'No problem,' and inside you wonder to yourself, Does she think that about me too? and that feels oppressive. And you go outside and you stand at the pedestrian crossing and you check yourself. And I hate myself for that.

Have you ever turned on the computer and you see videos of people who are just like you? In countries that are far away and countries that are not far away at all, they are being imprisoned and beaten and tortured and murdered and executed – because they are just like you.

And that feels oppressive.

Three weeks ago I was on television and I said that I believed that people who actively campaign for gay people to be treated less or treated differently are, in my gay opinion, homophobic. Now, some people – people who actively campaign for gay people to be treated less under the law – took great exception to that characterisation, and they threatened legal action against me and RTÉ. Now, RTÉ in its wisdom decided incredibly quickly to hand over a huge sum of money to make it all go away. I haven't been quite so lucky.

And for the last three weeks, I have been lectured to by heterosexual people about what homophobia is and who is allowed to identify it. Straight people have lined up – ministers, senators, barristers, journalists – have lined up to tell me what homophobia is and to tell me what I am allowed to feel oppressed by. People who have never experienced homophobia in their lives, people who have never checked themselves at a pedestrian crossing, have told me that unless I am being thrown into prison or herded onto a cattle train, then it is not homophobia, and that feels oppressive.

So now Irish gay people, we find ourselves in this ludicrous situation where we are not only not allowed to say publicly what we feel oppressed by, we're not even allowed to think it because the very definition, our definition, has been disallowed by our betters.

And for the last three weeks I have been denounced from the floor of the Oireachtas to newspaper columns, to the seething morass of internet commentary. Denounced for using 'hate speech' because I dared to use the word 'homophobia', and a jumped-up queer like me should know that the word 'homophobia' is no longer available to gay people. Which is a spectacular and neat Orwellian trick because now it turns out that gay people are not the victims of homophobia: homophobes are the victims of homophobia.

But let me just say that it's not true, because I don't hate you.

I do, it is true, believe that almost all of you are probably homophobes. But I'm a homophobe. It would be incredible if we weren't! To grow up in a society that is overwhelmingly and stiflingly homophobic and to somehow escape unscathed would be miraculous. So I don't hate you because you are homophobes. I actually admire you. I admire you because most of you are only a bit homophobic. And, to be honest, considering the circumstances, that is pretty good going.

But I do sometimes hate myself. I hate myself because I fucking check myself when standing at

pedestrian crossings. And sometimes I hate you
for doing that to me.

But not right now. Right now, I like you very
much for giving me a few moments of your time,
and for that I thank you.

When I had finished it was impossible for me to know
how it had been received. I felt like it had gone fine,
but they were a nice polite theatre audience – they were
unlikely to get up and walk out or start chatting among
themselves. At the end they responded enthusiastically
– there was even a standing ovation – but I was taking a
bow with the full cast of the show on the night of their final
performance so that was more than likely for them and
their two-hour performance, not my ten-minute speech.
I did notice that one of the actresses beside me seemed a
little teary and was squeezing my hand hard, but she was
taking a bow at the very end of a two-month run at the
national theatre so it was a big night for her. And when
the curtain came down and we walked offstage the other
actors congratulated me and said nice things, but that's
what performers do.

I made my way around to the front of the theatre to
meet Phillip and Ian, who said it was great, but that's what
friends do, and as we waited for a cab on the pavement
in front of the theatre some of the audience approached
me to say nice things, but that's what people do. Then
the cab pulled up, I jumped inside and went back to

Pantibar and threw myself into the show, spinning and sweating and telling silly stories for a lively Saturday-night bar crowd.

A few hours later in the wee hours of Sunday morning I got home, and while winding down before bed I turned on the computer and on Facebook I saw that someone had already posted a fuzzy video of my speech, filmed on a phone from the auditorium. The picture quality was poor, the sound was bad and the beginning of the speech was missing, yet it had already had a few hundred views, and by the time I woke up it had had a few thousand. I headed into town – it was the day of the protest against RTÉ's payout – and people mentioned it to me. They'd seen the fuzzy video online already. My friends joked about which of them had been the 'gay friend' on the train in the speech. (It was Veda.) Panti was working in the bar in the early evening, playing records, and when I checked the video on my phone a couple of times, the views were still going up. By the time they were reaching seven or eight thousand I was amazed but beginning to think we might have missed our chance to put up our own better-quality video. After all, surely there weren't many more than eight thousand people who'd want to watch it.

Conor called. He knew there was a video up already and he and Caroline had been trying to get theirs up all afternoon but there was a problem with the video shot by the second camera, and in the end, late on Sunday evening they put up a single-camera clip. It was a simply shot video of a drag queen giving a serious ten-minute speech about homophobia, and ten minutes is an eternity in YouTube terms. No one was going to watch it. And whoever the weird eight thousand people were who'd already watched the fuzzy version, well, they'd already seen it anyway. I was glad it was up online because I was happy with what I'd said and how I'd said it but, as far as I was concerned, that was the end of that.

But it was far from the end of that. It was only the beginning. The video immediately started racking up thousands of views and in the days that followed it spread like wildfire. It was being posted to blogs and Facebook pages all around the world, and when celebrities like Stephen Fry, Graham Norton, RuPaul and Martina Navratilova (Martina Navratilova!) tweeted it and said lovely things about it to their millions of followers, it spread even faster. I started getting emails from the UK, the US and Australia, and then it was picked up by the mainstream media. I started hearing clips of it coming from radios in taxis and my TV, and it was broadcast on stations as far away as France and Canada.

People were talking about it as a great oration, and the respected *Irish Times* critic and columnist Fintan O'Toole went so far as to say it was 'the most eloquent Irish speech since Daniel O'Connell was in his prime'. (I heard that Fintan was at my show some months later at the Galway International Arts Festival: having been assaulted by the kind of salacious stories I tell in my shows, he may now be regretting his words.) And the media storm that I had thought couldn't get any bigger exploded into a full-scale hurricane. Suddenly I was the hottest property in media, and every newspaper, every radio programme and every TV show wanted to talk to me.

And talk to them I did, because every interview was helping me to make noise and by now I was making a bloody racket. Foreign media started to come looking for me. I did satellite interviews with the BBC and Channel 4, I took part in a debate on BBC World, I did TV and print interviews for CNN, Reuters, the *Washington Post*, and one evening while I was eating cereal for dinner the phone rang and a voice said, 'Hi, this is Maureen Dowd from *The New York Times*,' and the racket just got louder.

The Archbishop of Dublin denounced homophobia and practically declared himself to be on 'Team Panti'. Neil Tennant called because the Pet Shop Boys had put the speech to music and made a video to go with it. Whole TV shows were devoted to debating homophobia and one prime-time politics show played the entire ten-minute speech before a panel debated the scandal. The solicitor who was acting for Iona and Waters appeared on that show, looking rattled, and Andrew was aghast, thinking it unseemly for a solicitor to discuss his clients' ongoing cases in public. The whole affair was debated in the Senate and raised in the European Parliament, and one bizarre afternoon I went out to RTÉ to be interviewed by Miriam

O'Callaghan (the 'nice TV lady' of the speech). After the recording we stood in the middle of the RTÉ newsroom, surrounded by the familiar faces of TV news reporters, and we all watched the live stream of the Dáil debate on 'Pantigate' (as it was now being called) on the newsroom television screens, as TDs denounced RTÉ, bandied my and Panti's names about, and demanded answers from the minister. It was a slightly surreal experience.

It was also the first real inkling I got of how the perception of me had changed. I had been out to RTÉ many times before and no one would pay me a blind bit of notice, but this time was different. I was at the centre of a media storm, a storm that RTÉ was part of, and I had gained a new kind of celebrity. People came over to me and many of them wanted to let me know they supported me. The director of radio made a point to come down and meet me, and the receptionist hadn't needed to ask me my name.

People started to stop me in the street. A middle-aged 'regular Dub' with a beer belly and a soccer jersey stopped me as I passed to shake my hand and tell me about his lesbian daughter, and while he was doing so, another man came up and asked if he could take a picture. An old lady at the milk fridge in Tesco turned to me and told me that 'that shower' didn't represent her. A man with two kids on Parnell Square pointed at me and said to his kids, 'That's boy Panti.' Everywhere I went people wanted to talk to me, shake my hand and

say, 'Fair play to ya.' A country mother came into the
bar in a nice floral dress, looked around, walked up to
me and said, 'I have a gay son – he's in Australia now –
and I wanted to thank you. Can I give you a hug?' She
hugged me and walked back out.

I spoke to my parents, who'd watched the speech and
were very proud. They'd starting hearing from relatives
and old friends who said nice things. People don't
usually say nice things to my parents about their drag-
queen son – and only a few days earlier my mother had
been upset because she couldn't 'read the paper without
seeing incorrect things about my son'.

Then people were shouting across the street that they
were 'Team Panti' and signs were appearing in shop
windows. There were T-shirts and bumper stickers and
graffiti, and eventually we started selling T-shirts in
the bar with the money going to the gay youth group.
Orders flooded in from all over the world. A group of
students 'infiltrated' the studio audience of a TV show,
and every time the camera cut to the audience you'd see
'Team Panti' T-shirts. Being on 'Team Panti' became a
way to say what kind of Ireland you wanted. It became
a way to protest against an Ireland we had thought we
had left behind but which had reared its ugly head again
– a censorious, interfering, repressed, backward-looking
Ireland. Being on 'Team Panti' was a way of saying you
rejected the kind of Ireland that Iona *et al* were trying to
drag us back to.

Of course, I was well aware that in many ways it had little or nothing to do with me. I mean, there would never have been shop-window mannequins dressed in 'Team Rory' T-shirts. There would never have been bumper stickers or restaurant receipts with 'Team Rory' printed on them, because Rory is a real person with an ordinary person's baggage. Rory has ex-boyfriends who are pissed off with him and a mother whose birthday he never remembers. But Panti has none of the messy baggage associated with being human. Panti doesn't poop. So it was easy for people to turn her into a symbol, an avatar. An avatar for the kind of Ireland they wanted. The kind of Ireland that would choose a drag queen for a kind of figurehead.

As the video kept spreading I was fielding more and more calls from around the world, and the emails kept arriving. And the letters and the cards and the flowers. And they just kept on coming. Thousands of them. And they were from all over. From Dublin and Galway and Letterkenny and Mullingar, and from Frankfurt and Melbourne and Buenos Aires and Chicago. They were from twelve-year-old girls and fifty-year-old bus drivers, from lesbians in Denmark, grandmothers in Australia and straight guys in Scotland. From all kinds of people. Some were from gay people writing to thank me for articulating what they felt, and others from their parents or brothers or sisters or friends, but many were writing to tell me their stories because, in a way that

I could never have imagined, all these different people related in some way to what I had said. Gay people, straight people, women, people in wheelchairs, fat kids in school, teenagers with Asperger's, and even a ginger-haired guy in London who was fed up having to check himself for being ginger! I even got a card that had fifty euro inside and a note that simply said, 'for the wig fund'. To get them and read them (or as many as I could) was wonderful and inspiring and occasionally devastating.

And I was standing in the middle of all this, tired and stunned, trying to work out exactly what the hell had just happened. Trying to remember how all of this had even started and how this thing, which had begun so worryingly and so distressingly, had become so bizarre and exhilarating. And fun.

Why the video had spread so far and wide, why so many people had watched it, still confounds me. After all, it's not exactly 'click-bait' material. It's not a twenty-second clip of a puppy falling off a sofa or a drunk guy trying to get his pants on – the kind of thing you see passed around online and think it might give you a quick giggle, the kind of thing that can rack up millions of views because it takes nothing to watch fifteen seconds of a kitten getting stuck in a cereal box. It's a ten-minute speech. About *homophobia*. Who the hell wants to watch that?

Of course I know from the response it got that it has a lot to do with what I said, and how I said it, and how many people related to it in some way. But there were other factors. That it was Panti on screen played a big role. Many fewer people would have clicked on a ten-minute speech that they could see was delivered by a guy in a shirt. No matter what you think of drag queens, we get your attention. That it was a glamorous, brightly lit, blonde-haired queen standing in front of four handsome actors, who were in the shadows dressed as downtrodden workers, played a role. The visual was important. Not only was it visually interesting, but it also added to what I said. It underscored what I said. And that it was titled a 'Noble Call' played a role. It's an evocative phrase and sets the video up to be taken seriously. It gives it a kind of gravitas before you've even clicked 'play'. All these small, unplanned, coincidental factors played a part in turning a ten-minute oration on the gay experience by a drag queen with badly brushed hair into a whole that was much greater than its constituent parts.

And although the white-hot heat of attention that followed the speech has died down, the effect of those ten minutes and the scandal that prompted it lingers.

It changed how people see me. For my entire career I have struggled against people's limited perception of drag queens, of what they are and can be, but that speech made people take me seriously. I wasn't just a clown in a dress, I was an 'orator'. I was *controversial drag queen Panti Bliss*'. I was somebody not to be taken lightly. If anything, people take me *too* seriously now!

They want me to be the perfect gay all the time, as if I represent every gay. They want me to be inspiring, when previously the only thing I ever inspired anyone to do was be tested for an STI! Sometimes people take everything I say so seriously that they are primed to be offended. I recently upset the Bisexual Network of Ireland by making a joke about bisexuals. It was a silly joke but they were hurt because *Panti* had said it. Panti, the inspiring LGBT rights warrior.

'Pantigate' gave me a level of recognition, a kind of fame, I hadn't had previously. Before Pantigate I was well known to the gay community, to clubbers, theatre types, media types, but almost overnight Panti became a household name. Now tabloids call wanting to know what an inspiring drag queen thinks of everything from Miley Cyrus to the Taoiseach's performance. Gay Byrne wants to hear my thoughts on *The Meaning of Life*. People on the kinds of radio programmes my mother listens to don't bother explaining who I am any more: they casually use my name and assume listeners know who I am.

And it pushed Rory into a spotlight I never wanted and am not entirely comfortable with. One of the great things about being a drag queen is being able to have a public persona entirely separate from the private one, and that suits me. However, in order to fight my corner during the whole débâcle, I needed to put Rory to the barricades too. I know that very quickly people will forget who Rory is and what I look like, and that will suit me fine, but in the aftermath of Pantigate it was an adjustment, and it's still odd to be standing at the hot deli counter paying for a jumbo sausage roll when a woman with a basket full of pumpkin seeds and rice crackers comes up to tell me how inspiring I am.

It's just weird. The audiences that come to my shows have changed, too, and now I see people who would never previously have come to watch a drag queen in the theatre. When I was writing my last show I found myself being affected by people's new expectations of me. I'd write a salacious joke, then find myself thinking, Panti can't say that! I had to make a conscious decision to go ahead and do the joke. To be who I've always been. Part of the appeal of drag, a large part of the reason I was drawn to it, is its inherently transgressive nature. Its discombobulating nature. Its underground, outsider origins.

There is a tension between that and the 'new Panti'. Can you still be transgressive and discombobulating when you are on the cover of *VIP* magazine and accepting awards from universities? Can you still be an outsider artist and do a 'Paint Along With Panti' event for kids in the garden of the Museum of Modern Art? It's a question I'm still working out the answer to.

Pantigate and the Noble Call have also given me new opportunities. I get invited to speak all over the country and around the world, and I'm still amazed and grateful that students in Montréal or gays in Berlin are interested in what I have to say. Venues that previously wouldn't have considered booking my show are now eager to have me, and I'm also grateful for that. And if it weren't for that Abbey speech you'd be reading *Fifty Shades of Grey* right now, not the ramblings of a middle-aged drag queen with 'notions', and for that I can only apologise.

At the height of Pantigate when I was doing the rounds of radio studios and reporters' Dictaphones, fighting for my reputation and struggling to get out from under the weight of solicitors' letters, part of my strategy was to level the playing field by personalising RTÉ. In Ireland people talk of RTÉ, the national broadcaster, as a kind of monolith. A powerful hive mind. It is seen as a big, powerful organisation that speaks with authority, and I knew that to be an entirely false impression. I knew that RTÉ was just a sprawling building full of regular people – some efficient, some smart, some inept, most of them nice. People who were just getting on with their jobs and wondering what to make for dinner.

But that's not how people see it. 'RTÉ' makes decisions, not some guy at a desk who just remembered he was supposed to pick the kids up from Irish dancing class ('Fuck!'). RTÉ 'issues statements', instead of a woman from Portarlington with a desk fan and a hangover, who answered the phone. And while I knew there were advantages in being seen as the plucky underdog, I also knew it was working against me. There was a perception that if RTÉ had caved in to the complainants' demands then surely they must have been right. That drag queen *must* have said something terrible. So I deliberately set out to bring RTÉ down to my size. To pull back the curtain and show the Wizard of Oz frantically twirling his knobs.

To do that I took every opportunity to ridicule RTÉ's legal department and point out the shortcomings of their advice – it wasn't hard. By any measure, the whole affair had been an unmitigated disaster for RTÉ. Their legal team had managed to turn a small, annoying kerfuffle into a PR catastrophe that ended up making their employers look spineless, and become the focus of anger, protests and ridicule. They gave RTÉ's commercial competitors the opportunity to pile on and give them a good kicking, created angry in-house tension between staff and management and, for good measure, destroyed the trust RTÉ had worked hard to build with the LGBT community.

My other strategy in interviews was to go around the important-sounding corporation 'RTÉ' straight to the ordinary-sounding Glen Killane, the managing director of television. I stopped talking about how RTÉ had treated me and spoke instead about how Glen Killane had treated me. I said I was looking for an apology for the attempt to throw me under the bus. I said I wasn't looking for a public apology and I wasn't interested in lawyers. A simple phone call would do. He should apologise, I said, because 'if he asked his mother what he should do, she'd tell him he should'. But I wasn't simply doing it as a fighting strategy. I also believed it. I *had* been treated badly by RTÉ and, no matter what the eventual outcome, I deserved an apology. And no doubt Glen Killane was under all sorts of pressure to make the decisions he did – and no doubt he was led awry by his legal advice – but he was the one holding the mishandled can. An apology from the cleaner wasn't going to cut it.

A few weeks after the media spotlight had moved on, Glen called and asked me to meet him for coffee. He didn't ask me to come out to RTÉ but said he'd come into town to meet me. I took that as a good sign. We met at a busy city-centre café and Glen joined the long queue to get the coffees. I took that to be a good sign too. I liked him. He seemed like a good guy. It just happened that we'd ended up on opposite sides of a shit-storm. We had a good chat. Explained each other's side of things, man to drag queen. We were never going to agree about some things but, as the kids say, 'We were good.'

As we stood up to leave and I was putting on my jacket, a young woman approached me. 'Sorry, I don't mean to interrupt,' she said, 'but I wanted to give you this.' She handed me a folded page torn from a notebook and walked away. Standing beside Glen, I opened it and written in pencil was a sweet note saying something nice about me, and declaring her to be on Team Panti.

I looked at Glen with a smirk. 'That happens all the time now.'

Epilogue

RuPAUL ONCE SAID, 'WE'RE BORN naked, the rest is drag,' and she's right. We all play different roles, presenting different versions of ourselves to different audiences. Parent, colleague, boss, friend, sibling, neighbour, adversary: all of them us, each different. Public faces and private faces that we dress accordingly. The polite woman who turns up at the parent-teacher meeting, in her nice blouse and her hair in a neat ponytail, is a very different person from the tired, bedraggled woman eating Jaffa Cake crumbs off her bobbled leggings in front of *EastEnders*. The crude bloke on the building site making wisecracks with his mates over today's page three is a very different guy from the charming boyfriend taking his new girlfriend out for a meal later. The silly face-pulling dad helping his daughter find her Dora the Explorer schoolbag in the morning is a different man from the sober-suited one sitting opposite his bank manager that afternoon. The serious, capable woman in the Monday-morning meeting is unrecognisable from the woman who was hanging over a balcony in a nightclub in Ibiza with a glass of vodka in her hand only two nights previously.

Drag queens do it too. It's just that our public faces are even more deliberate, more clearly defined, sharply delineated with lip-liner and eyebrow pencil. No less real, no less *us*, just packaged differently.

In a way, being a drag queen is like living two parallel lives. One you would recognise: it begins when a vet's wife holds her little gay baby in a Galway hospital and ends, I suspect, mundanely. The other, like a comet, appears suddenly and explodes across the nightlife sky in a shower of glitter and eyelashes. Its life is shorter, but burns more brightly. It is true to say that I breathed life into Panti, but it is equally true to say that she breathed life into *me*. She coloured me. She made me a better person – and somehow managed to pay my bills along the way while she was at it. Sure, she's brought me some trouble and a few heartaches over the years – attracting the attention of lawyers and scaring off a few boyfriends – but all of that pales in comparison to what she's given me. It was more than I could ever have imagined when I first pulled on a sticky dress made of surgical gloves in art college: friends, opportunities, courage, adventures, fun.

And, boy, it's been fun! I've tumbled off tabletops in crowded bars, and got first-aid tips from Diana Ross.

I've performed in the day ward of an old folks' home and in art galleries in Tokyo, on upturned beer crates in tiny basement bars and on huge floats in the St Patrick's Day parade. I've pushed Cyndi Lauper onstage in a wheelchair and been remixed by the Pet Shop Boys. I've performed sellout shows on the stages of grand venues and turned up at crappy nightclubs to discover they don't even have a stage. I've fallen into dressing rooms exhausted, in corset-induced agony, but howling with laughter. I've entertained in London, Melbourne and Paris, and horrified in Limerick, Derry and Hobart. And I wouldn't change a thing.

I don't know who or what I'd be without Panti, but I know I wouldn't be happier. She liberated me, and for that, I can only thank her.